VICTORIAN
BOOK
ILLUSTRATION

VICTORIAN BOOK ILLUSTRATION

The Technical Revolution

GEOFFREY WAKEMAN

DAVID & CHARLES: NEWTON ABBOT

0 7153 5936 3

Set in 11 on 13pt Imprint
and printed in Great Britain
by Fletcher & Son Ltd, Norwich
for David & Charles (Holdings) Limited
South Devon House Newton Abbot Devon

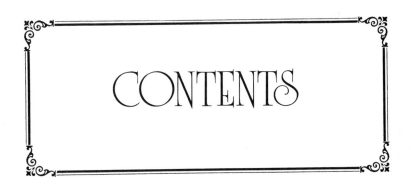

CONTENTS

LIST OF ILLUSTRATIONS

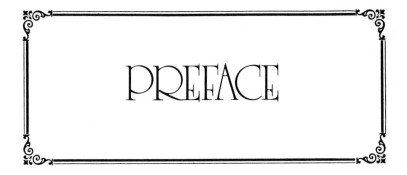

PREFACE

IT IS a matter of some contention whether the Victorian period forms a historical entity or not. But, so far as book illustration is concerned, it can at least be said that it saw the replacement of autographic methods of reproduction by photomechanical methods. This technical revolution is the subject of this book, which I have tried to confine to the period 1837–1900, although occasionally it has been necessary to stray outside these dates.

A great number of libraries have helped me by lending books and answering queries during the last few years, and I am most grateful. I am particularly indebted to the Bodleian Library for permission to investigate books in the stacks, and for the assistance I have received from the custodians of the John Johnson Collection. I am grateful to David Charman for taking the photographs for the plates, and to John Walton for reading the proofs. I have also gained much valuable information from antiquarian booksellers, both those who send me their catalogues and those whose stocks I have anonymously examined.

9

Chapter One

INTRODUCTION

BOOKS PUBLISHED at the start of the nineteenth century, particularly illustrated books, are physically very different from those published at the end—due to the development of printing during the century from a hand craft to a technology. All the significant steps in this progress were taken during Victoria's reign, which saw the invention of photography and electrotyping at its beginning, and the perfection of the cross-line screen near its end— three most important inventions in the printing of pictures.

A very large number of books were published during the Victorian period: in the late 1850s about 2,600 volumes were being published annually, by 1874 this had increased to 4,500 and by the end of the 1890s it was around 6,000. A fairly large proportion of these were illustrated, and any writer about nineteenth-century illustration must select those which seem most significant. Most writers have selected the artist as the most prominent figure in the production of an illustrated book, but without the printer there would be no book at all, and in a factual book the artist can often be only an impediment to the reader's appreciation of a particular place or artifact. All the important progress made in the printing of pictures during the Victorian period shows constant attempts to reduce the importance of the artist as an intermediary, and at the same time to reproduce the tones seen in nature. These features of illustration are the concern of this book. The inventions on which the new processes were based are well known, but the purpose here is to determine when they went into commercial use for book illustration, often a very different thing.

It would be pleasant to record that the more sophisticated illustrative methods of the 1880s and 1890s produced illustrations of higher artistic standards than those in use at the beginning of the Victorian period. But we cannot. It seems more likely that the reverse is true. There was no artist working at the end of the century of the stature of Turner, who was still producing book illustrations in the late 1830s. The only great book illustrator of the 1890s was Beardsley, who stands out from the general lush romanticism of the book illustration of his period, which generally reflects at a commercial level the work of such popular academic artists as Herkomer, Cope, Orchardson and Forbes.

The commercial exploitation of printing processes is dependent on its machinery—the press itself. The first breakthrough was the Stanhope press, with its iron platen the same size as the bed; by cutting out one of the two pulls necessary to print every page on the common press this must have increased productivity considerably. It is probable that most books were printed on flat-bed machines, either the two revolution or stop cylinder types, particularly after 1858 when the Wharfedale became available. The Miehle was first offered to the trade in 1887 and contributed to the development of three-colour work, combining considerable power with good register.[1]

Power-platen presses were in use from the early 1830s, when the Hopkinson & Cope double-platen machine became available, the first one being built in 1830 for Spottiswoode.[2] A much better machine was built by Napier slightly later—in its single-platen form it is mentioned in *A History of Wonderful Inventions* (Chapman & Hall, 1849) as having been 'recently constructed' (Plate 1). The Oxford University Press still had some similar machines in use as late as 1894,[3] having bought three in 1887. There is occasional evidence for the use of platen presses where the bolts of a book have not been cut and the pinholes can be seen.

Plate 1   Napier power platen press. *A History of Wonderful Inventions* (1849)

As late as 1897 Thomas Bolas[4] said that rotary machines were not much used for printing process blocks, and that, although a machine for printing photogravures was exhibited at the Printing Trades Exhibition in 1880, they were not really satisfactory.[5] Storey's of Lancaster were using rotary machines for their secret method of screened rotogravure by 1895, but this method was not much used in bookwork before the end of the century. The first effective lithographic power press was that of Sigl, dating from 1852, but it is unlikely that power presses were commonly used for lithography before the 1880s. Lithographic machine makers, as opposed to press makers, are first listed in Kelly's *Post Office Directory* as a separate trade in 1885.

Certain social developments had a direct bearing on the expansion of the nineteenth-century book trade. One of the most important was improved transport, particularly the railways, whose station bookstalls needed cheap books. A large number of reprints, and in some cases new books in series, are features of Victorian publishing. Some of them had titles that were quite explicit as to their aim—Routledge's 'Railway Library', for example. 'Yellow backs' were aimed at the same market, and provided a good living for the colour printers who produced their covers. The railways must also have contributed to the rise of large provincial printing houses, since they provided rapid communication with London and allowed the provincial printers to take advantage of lower wage rates when competing with London printers: examples in the field of illustration are Cowell's at Ipswich and Bemrose's at Derby. From 1872 until almost the end of the century the weekly wage for a compositor in London was 36s ($4.70), compared with 31s ($4.00) in Derby and 27s ($3.50) in Ipswich, according to Joseph Gould's *Letter-press Printer* in 1893. The wages of other operatives were doubtless in the same ratio.

Another technological advance that must have increased the sale of books was the improvement in lighting. Gaslighting, which had become general by the middle of the century in English towns,[6] was replaced in the last twenty years or so of the century by electric light. This led particularly to improvements in indoor photography, and illustrations in books of this period occasionally bear a caption saying the original was photographed by electric light. In the *Penrose Annual* for 1900 there is an advertisement for electric driving gear for printing presses.

The small size of firms, which is still one of the characteristics of the printing industry, applied particularly to picture printing: for instance, Orlando Jewitt and Edmund Evans were more typical of wood engravers than were the Dalziel Brothers. The larger printing firms—with a few exceptions, such as William Clowes, who used Knight's process, and Cowell, who took up anastatic printing—do not seem to have been innovators. Anyway, Knight had married a Clowes, and Cowell's were still small when they took up anastatic printing; as processes became more complicated it was easier for general firms to buy their illustrations (or blocks) from specialists than to produce their own.

Some idea of the growth in the photomechanical printing trades can be gained from the London directories. The numbers

TABLE I

THE PRINTING TRADES IN LONDON, 1852–1900

	1852	1862	1872	1876	1880	1885	1889	1893	1896	1900
Printers	367			1,086						1,511
Copper-plate printers	55	64		126	90	83	75	73	68	66
Lithographers	123	156		398	425	420	449	474	453	429
Photolithographers			5	14	22	29	35		33	29
Collotype printers								5	9	14
Engravers, photographic and automatic				1	8	13	36	39		
Photo-engravers									89	94
Process engravers								28		
Photo-zincographers									1	*4

* Three of these firms listed in 1896 as photo-engravers.

Sources: *Post Office London Trades Directory* (1852 and 1862); and Kelly's *Post Office Directory of Stationers, Printers, etc* (1872, 1876, 1880, 1885, 1889, 1893, 1896, 1900).

of the firms have been listed in Table 1. There was a steady rise in the number of letterpress printers from 367 in 1852 to 1,511 in 1900. The lithographers expanded rapidly around the middle of the century, and it is surprising to find copper-plate printers also expanding until the last quarter of the century, until one remembers that most printers did not rely on bookwork but were employed on jobbing or various specialist printing. Photolithographers are not listed as a separate trade before the specialised directories of the book trade began to appear in 1872:

the first five firms listed were James Akeman, J. Leitch & Company, Vincent Brooks Day & Son, Maclure & Macdonald, and Edward Stanford. Collotype printers are first listed separately in 1893, twenty years after collotype was first used commercially: the firms listed are John R. Gotz, The Graphotone Company, W. H. Griggs, Hazell Watson & Viney, and the London Stereoscopic & Photographic Company. One name obviously missing from this list is the Autotype Company, a reminder that the directories are not very accurate. The classification varied from one edition to another, so that the eighty-nine photo-engravers who suddenly appeared in 1896 largely comprised those previously listed as 'automatic and photographic engravers' and 'process engravers'.

From time to time in this book references are made to various methods of illustration coming into use or falling out of fashion, but, since it has been impossible to examine all the Victorian books, these references are based on a sample of those published between 1850 and 1900. The sample consisted of all the books in the Bodleian Library classified under 'art', a classification only started in 1850, which is why the sample starts at that date and not 1837. Details of this sample and the figures that emerged are given in the Appendix.

Chapter Two
BEFORE THE GREAT EXHIBITION

WOOD ENGRAVING

BY THE early years of Victoria's reign wood engraving was well established as a method of commercial book illustration, the number of London firms engaged in it having increased from the fourteen listed in Johnstone's *London Guide* of 1817 to twenty-four in the *Post Office Directory* of 1842. As greater prosperity followed the depression in the book trade of the late 1820s and the 1830s, the number of firms increased more rapidly and the 1852 *Post Office Directory* lists forty-seven. The considerable increase in work represented by this growth must have been partly due to the illustrated periodicals, which are a feature of publishing at this time, as well as the lavishly illustrated number books like Knight's *Old England*, 1845.

According to one of the most able wood engravers of the second half of the century, W. J. Linton, the period from 1790 to 1835 saw English wood engraving at its best. The start of this period is dominated by Bewick, but it also includes work by George

Plate 2   Wood engraving by J. Thompson. Advertisement leaf for
Yarrell's *History of British Birds* (1843). 8 × 8·5cm

Cruikshank and William Harvey, and such admirable books as
Major's *Complete Angler*, 1823. Linton thought most highly of
John Thompson, who had been a pupil of Robert Branston, a
contemporary of Bewick but belonging to the London school of
reproductive engravers. Some of the illustrations in *Puckle's Club*,
printed by John Johnson in 1817, are Thompson's work, but he
can be seen at his best in William Yarrell's *History of British
Birds*, 1843 (Plate 2). This book was published by John Van
Voorst, who was responsible for a number of books well illustrated
with wood engravings, including the only two books in which
Constable's work was reproduced in this medium during the
Victorian period—Gray's *Elegy*, 1839 (Plate 3) and *The Seven*

Plate 3 Wood engraving after Constable for Gray's *Elegy*. Advertisement leaf issued by Van Voorst (1837). 6 × 8cm

Ages of Shakespeare, 1840.[1] The engravers were T. Bagg and W. H. Powis. Thompson's last important work was cutting fourteen of the blocks for Tennyson's *Poems*, published by Moxon in 1857, the work being shared with Linton, the Dalziels and others. The system of using different firms to cut blocks for one book was quite common throughout the century, probably to speed up the process.

Some attractive books were produced towards the end of the great period of wood engravers, such as James Ingram's *Memorials of Oxford*, 1837, in which W. A. Delamotte's drawings were engraved by Orlando Jewitt. Wood engraving lends itself to the small illustration that can be printed with the letterpress and produce a harmonious whole in book design. Its decline can be seen in J. G. Lockhart's *Ancient Spanish Ballads*, 1842, though this book is a second edition in which extra care was devoted to the production in special endpapers and binding. Some of the wood blocks are vignetted, but others are full-page plates inserted into the book sideways on, thus fully divorcing them from the text. In Dudley Costello's *A Tour through the Valley of the Meuse*, 1845, the same decline can be seen: although the engravings were made by Henry Vizetelly and in many cases appear at the chapter heads, some of them have been placed at odd positions in the text and bled into the letterpress in such a way as to reduce its width to a very narrow measure; and although in many ways this is an attractive book it shows the beginning of that lack of feeling for the printed page that was to bedevil illustration throughout the Victorian period.

Some authors appreciated the way in which wood engravings could be printed with the text, and Dickens planned their exact placing in some of his works. Some of his proofs for *Master Humphrey's Clock*, for instance, have survived with his directions for the insertion of the blocks.[2]

In making wood engravings it was first necessary to draw or transfer the picture on to a prepared wood block, generally made of box for bookwork. If any areas were to print less heavily than the rest, their surfaces were worked over with a mezzotint rocker to lower them. The picture was then redrawn and the engraver cut away the wood with a steel graver, while the block rested on a sand-filled leather pad (Plates 4/5).

Plate 4 Wood engraving tools from T. Gilks, *The Art of Wood Engraving* (1866). 9 × 8·5cm

Stereotypes had been used increasingly since about 1830 to duplicate wood engravings.[3] There were two methods in use: one was the plaster of paris method invented by Lord Stanhope, in which a cast was taken of the block and then used as a mould into which the type metal was poured; and the other was known as clichage, in which the block was allowed to fall face downwards on to the metal when it was just sufficiently molten to receive an impression from which the casting was made. The metal used to make the mould in the second method had a

Plate 5   Wood engraver at work, from T. Gilks,
The Art of Wood Engraving (1866). 7 × 7cm

greater proportion of antimony in its composition than the
stereotype metal, giving it a higher melting point and so preventing matrix and cast from adhering. Although clichage appears
to have a number of obvious disadvantages, it was still used,
though rarely, as late as the 1890s.[4] After the mid-century a
better method using papier maché as the moulding material was
available, though by that time electrotyping was preferred for
high-grade work.

ETCHING

In addition to wood engraving a number of other methods of
illustration were in use when Victoria's reign began, and these
are generally classified as intaglio and planographic, the latter
being restricted at this time to lithography. Intaglio illustrations
are made from plates in which the ink lies in furrows below their
surface, which is wiped clear of ink before the impression is
taken. There are various ways of making the furrows in the

plate, and these ways may be used either on their own or in combination; to a certain extent each method produces characteristics that distinguish it from the others. It is customary to refer to an intaglio illustration by its most distinguishing feature, though this is often only part of the process by which the plate was made. Plates of copper or steel could be etched or engraved.

To make an etching the surface of the plate was first covered with an etching ground, for which there were various recipes. That used by Wilson Lowry and recommended by T. H. Fielding[5] was made of asphaltum, Burgundy pitch and white virgin wax melted together and tied up in a piece of stout silk cloth. The plate was warmed and the ground rubbed on it, the heat causing it to melt sufficiently to run out of the silk. The surface of the plate was then blackened by holding it inverted over the flame of a candle or some wax tapers twisted together. The picture was then copied on to tracing paper with a pencil, and the tracing placed face down on the plate. When both were passed through a rolling press, the image appeared reversed on the plate in fine silvery lines. The picture was then drawn through the ground with a series of etching needles, made of steel with various thicknesses of point; when the etcher had finished, the bared lines were bitten away with dilute nitric acid if the plate was copper. Etching on steel was established as a practicable working method by about 1824, when Edmund Turrell invented a corrosive medium of nitric acid, pyroligneous acid and alcohol[6] that would bite deeply instead of widely. The advantage of steel over copper was the very long run that could be printed from the plate.

Although etching was never a major illustration process, some very considerable artists used it, the greatest probably being George Cruikshank, who was at the height of his powers in the early Victorian period. From 1837 to 1843 he illustrated *Bentley's Miscellany*, a magazine that was reissued in book form in 1885 as *Old Miscellany Days*. Bentley paid him £50 over and above his fees for the plates for the use of his name (Plate 6). He is perhaps best known in this field for his illustrations to *Oliver Twist*,

Plate 6   Etching by George Cruikshank from *Old Miscellany Days*
(1885); originally published in 1838. It illustrates a story in which
the sailor objects to the showman's portrayal of the battle and sinks
the French fleet with oranges. 12 × 10cm

1837–9, Harrison Ainsworth's *The Tower of London*, 1840,[7] and
The Ingoldsby Legends, 1840–7.

Another illustrator of *The Ingoldsby Legends* was John Leech
(Plate 7), best remembered perhaps for his etchings to Surtees's

Plate 7   Etching by Leech. *The Ingoldsby Legends* (1840–7).
11·5 × 9cm

sporting novels, such as *Mr Sponge's sporting tour*, 1853, and
Handley Cross, 1854, hand-coloured in the tradition of sporting
prints. Hand-colouring, of course, increased the cost of the
plates, and books containing them were generally from half as
much again to twice the cost of uncoloured copies. W. M.
Thackeray's *Dr Birch and His Young Friends*, 1849, illustrated

DOCTOR BIRCH
& his
young friends.

by
M^r. M. A. Titmarsh

London: Chapman & Hall, 186, Strand.
1849.

Plate 8   Soft ground etching by Thackeray. Title-page spread
from *Dr Birch and His Young Friends* (1849). 15 × 21cm

A young Raphael.

with the author's own soft ground etchings, cost 5s plain or 7s 6d coloured (Plate 8).

Etching received an impetus towards the end of the century from the movement known as the painter etchers, and this is reflected in book illustration. The originator of the movement is said to have been Charles Jacque,[8] and its most important artist J. M. Whistler, who influenced F. Seymour Haden, a relation by marriage. Although the latter made some etched book illustrations—two plates in William Bemrose's *Joseph Wright*, 1885, for example—the most influential book illustrator was P. G. Hamerton, who wrote a number of books recommending etching for book illustration and edited the *Portfolio*, which was illustrated in this way. This English revival of etching had been influenced by the French, whose greatest practitioner was Charles Meryon—important in that his work led to a school of architectural etching in England.[9] It is not uncommon to find topographical books and books of architecture of the 1880s and 1890s illustrated with etchings—for example, Andrew Lang's *Oxford*, 1882 (Plate 9). The most attractive etched illustrations from this period are Samuel Palmer's in Virgil's *Eclogues*, 1883, and Milton's *Minor Poems*, 1888. The former has five etchings and nine photogravures of designs for etchings, and the latter is entirely illustrated with heliogravures by Dujardin. An interesting example of graphic work produced by a publisher of books (as opposed to a publisher of prints) is the *Oxford Almanac*, which generally reflected in a conservative way the fashion in book illustration: etchings were used in 1878, 1881, 1885–6, 1889, 1892, 1893 and 1902.

RULING MACHINES AND MEDAL ENGRAVING

It is paradoxical that etching, which allows great freedom of line to the artist, should have been used so much during the nineteenth century for the production of parallel lines. These lines were for the most part used to obtain tones in the style of illustration generally described as engraving, and were produced by what are known as ruling machines, though they were hand-operated devices more in the nature of simple drawing instruments. Their

Plate 9   Etching from *Oxford* by A. Lang (1882). 21 × 16·5cm

inventor seems to have been Wilson Lowry, whose first machine, dating from 1790, was improved in 1798 when he invented the diamond point to replace the steel etching needle, and by 1799 was capable of drawing lines to a point or describing concentric circles.[10] The machines consisted of a base plate over which was fixed a ruler supported at both ends. A sliding socket carrying an etching needle was fitted to the ruler. The plate to be etched went under the ruler, after the ground had been laid, and was held down on it by a spring. The ruler could be moved, generally by a screw mechanism, to enable the parallel lines to be marked through the ground. In addition to becoming more elaborate as the century wore on, ruling machines were also applied to lithographic and relief printing (Plate 10).

During the second half of the nineteenth century numerous patents were filed for pantographs and enlarging machines, but there is little evidence for their use in book illustration. One

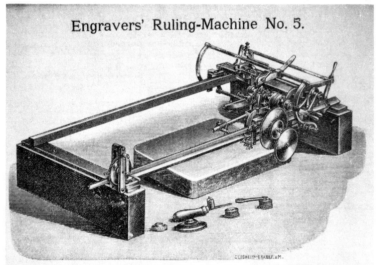

Plate 10   Ruling machine from Klimsch & Co's catalogue (1892)

was invented by Isaac Taylor,[11] whose plates illustrated Robert Traill's translation of the *Jewish Wars* of Josephus, 1848–50. It is said that Taylor lost money on his very complicated machine, though it was capable of giving effective halftones.

One common application of ruling machines to book illustration was in medal engraving, a method of producing facsimiles of medals that had a lifelike appearance of relief on the page; the first practicable machines were built in America in the early years of the century, and they had also been made in France and England before the Victorian period. The French machine was built by Achille Colas and used in England for the plates in *The Great Seals of England*, Hering, 1837, and H. F. Chorley's *The Authors of England*, 1838. Some copies of the latter have an account of the process and its invention bound up at the back.[12] John Bate patented a machine in London in 1832 and named his process anaglyptography; it was used to illustrate Captain William Siborne's *History of the War in France and Belgium in 1815*, 1844 (Plate 11).

The method of operation was to clamp the medal (or a cast of it) down to the machine, and move a tracing arm across it. The relief on the surface of the medal raised or lowered the tracer and this motion was transmitted to an etching needle, which moved across a metal plate in a similar manner. The etcher thus produced a line representing the relief of a section of the original. When one line had been made, the tracer and etcher were moved a little sideways and another section was drawn, the relief of the medal thus being built up in a series of lines. Medal engravings were sometimes electrotyped and printed in relief, as was done on the title-page of the second edition of A. Smee's *Elements of Electrometallurgy*, 1843.

ENGRAVING

Closely associated with etching was engraving. For the first twenty years or so of the century copper was the metal most commonly used for this method of illustration, continuing the tradition of copper-engraved plates in eighteenth-century books.

Plate 11 Medal engraving from W. Siborne's *History of the War in France and Belgium in 1815* (1844). 17 × 8cm

Copper engraving was principally used for reproductive work, a practice that continued in the nineteenth century. Intaglio plates, however, suffer from two disadvantages for book illustration: they are difficult to integrate with a text printed in relief, and they are expensive. Copper plates were generally first etched, and then gone over with a graver of lozenge cross-section to produce lines of varying width and depth.

Before printing, the plate was warmed on a stand over a brazier filled with charcoal, later replaced by a spirit lamp, and later still by gas heating, introduced by Thomas Brooker about 1840. The plate was then printed on a rolling press. At the start of the century the presses were made of wood, and long levers acted directly on the rollers, but wood was replaced by iron probably well before the Victorian period, and iron presses were operated by a gear train linked to a flywheel. Woollen blankets were used to press the paper firmly into the incised lines in the plate, the surface of the plate being wiped free of ink so that the ink remaining in the lines would print under pressure. The constant wiping of the plate and the considerable pressure to which it was subjected in printing meant that copper plates wore out after about 4,000 good impressions had been obtained.[13]

Copper was used very little for engraved book illustration after 1837, steel replacing it during the 1820s and early 1830s. A number of inventors had worked on the use of steel for engraving, and the method eventually adopted by the majority of steel engravers was that first introduced in the early 1820s by Albert Warren. By the middle of the century plates of uniform consistency and not subject to warping could be supplied $\frac{8}{100}$ in thick, and any degree of hardness required by the artist could be supplied.[14]

By the 1830s English steel engraving was widely recognised in Europe as outstanding, largely because watercolour landscapes of one of the greatest English artists, J. M. W. Turner, were being reproduced in this medium.[15] Turner often made his watercolours with the engraver in mind, and his intentions were brilliantly executed by such engravers as W. B. Cooke, W. Miller and E. & W. Finden. Nearly all Turner's work was published before 1837, however, though Thomas Campbell's *Poetical Works*, which he illustrated, was published in that year. It is among his best books and is almost as attractive as his work for Samuel Rogers's *Italy*, 1830, and *Poems*, 1834. Turner was undoubtedly the greatest artist to have his work reproduced in books in the form of steel engravings, but, considering his dates, he cannot really be claimed as a Victorian illustrator.

Very many other capable artists, however, were represented in this way. James Ingram's *Memorials of Oxford*, 1837, has plates by F. Mackenzie, a well-known topographical artist of his day, engraved by John Le Keux. There is more than accuracy about these engravings, to which artist and engraver have imparted the atmosphere of Oxford as it must have been when it was a quiet country town, with sheep and cows wandering down St Giles in the evening sunshine. In the field of natural history Sir William Jardine's *Naturalist's Library*, 1834–43, had steel plates engraved by W. H. Lizars and coloured by hand (Plate 12).

The great spate of books illustrated with steel engravings

Plate 12 Steel engraving by Lizars. W. Jardine, *The Naturalist's Library* (1834–43). Original hand coloured. 9 × 15cm

during the 1830s led to a decline in the art in the 1840s, which was also attributed by T. H. Fielding[16] to the low prices at which the prints were sold and particularly to the plethora of annuals. He states that when steel engraving first came into use the whole of the work was done with the burin, but it soon became the custom to etch a great deal of it and only finish it by engraving. In consequence, a good deal of the tone would be drawn with the ruling machine, and this undoubtedly contributed to the aesthetic and commercial decline of steel engraving in the second half of the century. It might be thought that after the introduction of acierage (steel facing) in the 1860s steel as an engraving surface would have been abandoned in favour of copper, but this does not seem to have happened in book illustration. In the 1880s the process of making a steel engraving was very similar to that of the 1840s: the illustration was transferred to the etching ground and etched before being finished with the burin; the ruling machine was used to etch in one set of lines and the plate regrounded before the cross lines were added. A book called *The Graphic Arts*, published by P. G. Hamerton in 1882, includes an example of engraving done in the manner of the 1830s, without using a ruling machine. Hamerton states that although machines were used in cheaper engravings they were not used 'in the very finest'. It is doubtful whether any of the finest engravings appeared in books, since, as Hamerton says, it might take several years to make one.

Steel engravings continue to be found as book illustrations almost to the end of the century, and the *Oxford Almanac* was engraved on steel from 1832 to 1870. During the 1870s Virtue, Spalding & Co published a series of monographs on artists, each illustrated with fifteen to twenty steel engravings· J. Dafforne's *Pictures of Sir A. W. Calcott, R.A.*, for example, was published in 1875 at 2s; *The National Gallery of British Art* was still coming out, apparently in parts, as late as 1897, though it consisted of prints from plates made many years previously. Virtue's had a considerable stock of old plates, having specialised in steel-plate books since the 1830s, when they had published the celebrated topographical books illustrated by W. H. Bartlett—*Switzerland*, 1836, *Scotland*, 1838, *The Danube*, 1844, and such works as Miss Pardoe's *Beauties of the Bosphorus*, 1840. George Virtue, founder of the firm, is said to have issued over 20,000 copper and steel engravings, and the firm was advertising this stock in Kelly's *Post Office Directory . . . of the . . . Printing Trades* in 1872.

MEZZOTINT

A popular method of intaglio reproduction in the last quarter of the eighteenth century (though invented in the seventeenth) was mezzotint. T. H. Fielding, describing it in 1841, wrote: 'The process of mezzotint consists in passing over a plate of steel or copper with an instrument called a cradle, by which a *burr* is raised on every part of the surface in such quantity, that if filled in with ink and printed the impression would be one mass of the deepest black. On the plate so prepared the lights and middle tints are burnished or scraped away, leaving it untouched for the darkest shades.' The outline was generally etched lightly before grounding the plate and more deeply when all the tones had been put in. Mezzotints on copper wore very rapidly owing to the constant wiping of the plate, so, as the number of copies in an edition increased, they became less and less suitable for book illustrations. At their best they were more used for collections of prints than for the illustration of books.

Steel was first used for mezzotinting by William Say in 1820,[17] and he was followed by T. G. Lupton and David Lucas. It was possible to obtain only some 1,500 good impressions, and steel could not give the rich tones that were so highly prized in mezzotints on copper. Steel was used for David Lucas's reproductions in John Constable's *English Landscape Scenery*, 1855, which consists of plates only. Turner's *Harbours of England*, 1856, was illustrated in this way by Thomas Lupton, and was reprinted a number of times while the plates became increasingly worn. For the last edition in 1895 they were reproduced by photogravure.

AQUATINT

In the late 1770s aquatint had been introduced into England and used very successfully for the illustration of expensive books. It was an etching method that produced a reticulated pattern whose density could be varied according to the depth to which the plate was bitten. It gave very good tonal effects, and, combined with hand-colouring, was a successful way of reproducing water-colours. It declined rapidly in popularity during the 1830s and was little used in the Victorian period, though odd examples occur—*Dr Syntax's Second Tour*, with plates by Rowlandson was still being marketed in a remainder binding as late as 1841;[18] T. H. Fielding's *On the Theory of Painting*, 1842, has some aquatints; and C. R. Cockerell's *Temple of Jupiter Panhellenius*, published by Weale, has one as late as 1860.

LITHOGRAPHY

Lithography was first used in England very early in the century, but did not become popular for book illustration until the 1820s. By the end of the 1830s it was in common use, being employed in some very attractive books like John Britton's *Drawings of the London and Birmingham Railway*, 1839, with illustrations by John Cooke Bourne. It depends for its effect upon the antipathy between grease and water: a greasy image on a surface of smooth limestone is first moistened and then inked; the image repels the water but accepts the ink, while the stone accepts the water and consequently repels the ink. The image can then be printed on paper by passing stone and paper through a scraper press, which gives a picture in black on a white background. By 1837 it was becoming common practice to add the impression of another stone, printed in a straw colour to give a tinted background, and this produced what are known as tinted lithographs.[19] In England they were developed by C. J. Hullmandel, who was the most important lithographer working in England in the earlier part of the century. The main developments in the 1830s were towards colour printing by lithography, and significant results were being achieved as Victoria's reign opened. Lithographs printed in colour are called chromolithographs, and the beginnings of their use in book illustration can be seen in the coloured plates in the early parts of Owen Jones's *Alhambra* in 1836, printed by Jones with the assistance of Louis Haghe and William Day.[20] It seems likely that Haghe & Day were the first to supply chromolithographed illustrations for a complete book in England, for (Sir) John Wilkinson's *Manners and Customs of the Ancient Egyptians*, 1837, has lithographs printed in colour signed 'Day and Haghe, printers to the King'. This work represents the start of an uninterrupted series of many books with chromolithographed plates.

Both the *Alhambra* plates and those in the *Ancient Egyptians* are printed in flat colours. An attempt at tone was made in the latter by slight stippling, and the use of zigzag lines to obtain a lighter effect. Blue and yellow were overprinted to make the green areas. The plates in a second series of the *Ancient Egyptians* in 1841 were issued in a supplementary volume: there are two chromolithographed fold-out plates, one 54cm long and the other 81cm (both on paper 23cm high). Both are in flat colours, and the green is printed from a separate stone except for a small area on one plate.

In 1844 John Weale started publishing *Quarterly Papers in Architecture*, which ran until 1845, and this has a number of chromolithographs by Owen Jones, Standidge & Co, and C. F. Cheffins. Some of Jones's plates indicate tone by using a black key stone in the chalk style, a method Cheffins also used but applied to a brown tint stone as well. Jones does not seem to have been entirely confident of producing toned chromolithographs at this time; his *Illuminated Calendar for 1845* has flat colour-printing in the borders and hand-coloured chalk-style lithographs for the pictorial plates. In the 1846 *Calendar*, however, the whole of the plates were chromolithographed. By 1848, when he printed *Flowers and Their Kindred Thoughts*, Jones had achieved a satisfactory method of printing tones, though in some of his later work he returned to the flat-colour style: it was used in many of the plates in *The Grammar of Ornament*, 1856, and in some of his gift-book work like *Joseph and His Brethren*, 1865, where it is very effective. C. J. Hullmandel was also attempting to print in colour by lithography in the late 1830s. In monochrome lithography he was constantly looking for ways of increasing the tonal effects: he had developed the stump style and was to patent lithotint in 1840.[21] His earliest colour printing appeared in *Colour as a Means of Art* by Frank Howard, published in 1838. The preface states that the method of printing the plates was due to a recent improvement in lithography by Hullmandel: 'It is capable of producing more nearly the effects of painting than any other style of engraving; but from these plates, professing only to represent masses of colour and general tone, and being the first that have been attempted in this particular application, they are not calculated to display Mr Hullmandel's improvement to advantage.' They are not very attractive and are not improved by the clumsy application of hand-colouring. The book was probably a failure, and it is not surprising to find it appearing in 1849 under the imprint of Henry Bohn, who specialised in remainder publishing. The plates appear to be basically tinted lithographs printed in straw, dark brown and blue, with the darkest colour stippled to make a key stone. Perhaps it was the style of work that made Hullmandel omit a black outline, which contributes to the illustrations' rather fuzzy appearance (Plate 13).

There is no doubt that he was searching for tonal effect, which he achieved not so much satisfactorily as magnificently in T. S. Boys's *Picturesque Architecture in Paris, Ghent, Antwerp, Rouen* in 1839. A Descriptive Notice by the publisher remarks significantly: 'This is the first and as yet the only attempt to imitate pictorial effects of landscape architecture in chromolithography, and . . . it has been carried so far beyond what was required in copying polychrome architecture, hieroglyphics, arabesques, etc., that is has become almost a new art. In most decorative subjects the colours are positive and opaque, the tints flat, and the several hues of equal intensity throughout, whereas

Plate 13 Chromolithograph by Hullmandel with hand colouring added. F. Howard, *Colour as a Means of Art* (1838). 9 × 7cm

in these views the various effects of light and shade, of local colour and general tone, result from transparent and graduated tints.' Clearly this refers to the efforts of Day & Haghe and Owen Jones. Hullmandel did not go on to exploit his method to any great extent, possibly because it was expensive—*Picturesque Architecture* sold at 8 guineas.

A few other printers worked in chromolithography during the 1840s. The best known firm is M. & N. Hanhart, who printed the plates in A. W. Pugin's *Glossary of Ecclesiastical Ornament and Costume*, 1844, as well as those in a number of other books in this decade, and continued to produce chromolithographs for many years.

The drawbacks of limestone as a printing surface were its weight and liability to break if clumsily handled, and for many years the only practicable alternative was zinc, which seems to have come into commercial use in England around 1830.[22] It is hardly possible to tell by looking at a lithograph whether it is printed from zinc, unless it is mentioned on the drawing. An example is the hand-coloured zincograph of St Christopher in Weale's *Quarterly Papers in Architecture* for March 1844, which is signed 'Zinco, 70, St Martin's Lane', the address of A. Ducôté. There is another example in Fielding's *Art of Engraving*, printed by Day & Haghe.

RELIEF PRINTING IN COLOUR

Although earlier attempts had been made to illustrate books in colour by relief printing, commercial work in this field really started with the prints of George Baxter, who patented his method in 1835 (No 6916). He normally used a key plate, engraved, aquatinted or lithographed and supplied the colours from engraved wood or metal blocks. For the most part his plates were used only as frontispieces, though a few books have more. Baxter was a skilful printer and his work is generally of a very high standard. Robert Mudie's *Summer*, 1837, has a very attractive frontispiece of Lake Maggiore and a decorative title page with a delightful vignette of a butterfly. The key is printed in dark blue and appears to be lithographed. In Humboldt's *Views of Nature*, 1850, an aquatint key was used for the frontispiece, a view of Chimborazo. Both these plates have Baxter's imprint stating that they were printed in oil colours, one which generally appears on his book illustrations. When it is considered that all printers at that time used oil-based ink, it may seem odd to emphasise this particular feature, but Baxter thought of his invention as a method of colouring plates and must have put this caption on to ensure that they were not mistaken for hand-coloured plates, in which watercolour was normally used.

Since most of Baxter's output was devoted to the print market, a more interesting printer so far as colour in bookwork is concerned is Charles Knight, who took out a patent (No 7673) in 1838. His method required the use of a modified Ruthven press or a specially built press, and, according to Sir Francis Bond Head,[23] the modified Ruthven press was in use at Clowes' print-

Plate 14 Knight's process. *Old England's Worthies* (1847). 25 × 17·5cm

ing works in 1840. The paper was placed in the bed of the press, and four hinged platens, each with a block mounted on its underside and inked with the appropriate colour in turn, were impressed on the paper by being folded inwards. The first examples of Knight's method appeared in Jackson & Chatto's *Treatise on Wood Engraving*, 1839, and are printed in four colours, or black and three colours. Where overprinting occurs it is dark brown on russet or light brown. The first use in book form was in W. Hughes's *Illuminated Atlas of Scripture Geography*, published by Knight in 1840 and containing twenty colour-printed maps, some of them rather muddy in appearance, possibly due to overprinting. They seem to be printed from about eight blocks each. Some copies of Jackson & Chatto's *Treatise* have one of these maps in place of the print entitled 'A café in Constantinople'. The second book in which the prints appear is probably the *Pictorial Museum of Animated Nature* [1844], which has a coloured frontispiece in each of its two volumes. The best known and most lavish use of the maps is in *Old England*, 1844–5, and *Old England's Worthies*, 1847 (Plate 14), which have twenty-four and twelve plates respectively. Knight called them 'Illuminated engravings' in a note in the first volume of *Old England*. He claimed that his method gave superior register, because the paper did not have to be removed from the press after every impression, and that up to sixteen consecutive impressions could be applied. John Kitto's *The Pictorial Sunday Book*, 1845, has twelve of the maps from Hughes's *Scripture Geography* (Plate 15) and a coloured frontispiece. The prints seem to have been very cheap to produce, for Head stated that the maps could be sold for 4½d each. If the number of copies of *Old England* which appear for sale is any indication, very large editions must have been printed, since it is a very common book.

The Pictorial Gallery of Arts, published in two volumes in 1847, has three colour plates, and an interesting section with wood engraved illustrations on printing. It was reprinted on better paper and republished as *The Arts and Industries of All Nations*, with a different Knight print as the frontispiece in

Plate 15 Knight's patent illuminated maps. J. Kitto, *The Pictorial Sunday Book*. 22 × 30cm

volume 2 (volume 1 has a hand-coloured lithograph) and a number of steel plates added. It is undated but certainly later than 1857, as one of the steel plates depicts an incident from the Indian Mutiny, and is possibly related to the 1862 Exhibition. About the time that the tinted lithograph became popular it is noticeable that tinted wood engravings also appeared, possibly as the relief printers' answer to the challenge of the former. Henry Vizetelly was responsible for a number of them; they were used in *Ancient Spanish Ballads*, 1841, and as the decorative title and frontispiece of Dudley Costello's *A Tour through the Valley of the Meuse* [1845]. Two tint blocks were used in the *Tour*, brown and blue, and hand-colouring was added. A similar technique can be seen in Mrs Percy Sinnett's *A Story about Christmas in the Seventeenth Century*, 1846.

Tinted wood engravings, however, were never as widely used as tinted lithographs, nor was colour printing from wood blocks ever as popular as chromolithography. Although some of Baxter's apprentices set up as colour printers, and he started selling licences to work his patented process in 1849, colour printing in relief really came into its own only after the Great Exhibition.[24]

The Victorian period of book illustration was one of constant change and experiment that had revolutionised the appearance of books by the 1890s. Most of the experiments and inventions found little use but were significant nonetheless, since it was in a climate of experiment that the important discoveries were enabled to flourish. One of the inventions that fell by the wayside was Godfrey Woone's patented process of 1837, later called gypsography, which involved making a drawing through plaster mounted on a metal base, and then casting a stereotype plate, using the plaster as the mould, and printing in relief. Robert Branston's son Robert illustrated Loudon's *Arboretum et Fruticetum Britannicum*, 1838, with blocks that were metal casts made from ordinary etchings; they had to be ground down to give a level surface for printing and were quite successful artistically. Another inventor was a lithographer named Louis Schoenberg, who issued Addison's *Spectator* in 1841 with illustrations printed by a process he called acrography. He never explained how it worked, but W. J. Stannard in his *Art Exemplar* stated that the printing surface was a metal block cast from the drawing, which was made by scratching away a white composition spread on glass or lithographic stone.[25]

Chapter Three

THE GREAT EXHIBITION

THE GREAT EXHIBITION of 1851 was unique in bringing together all the important branches of industry on an international scale. It also divides the century into two convenient historical periods, and marks the end of the beginning of Victoria's reign. Before the Exhibition life seemed not entirely committed to industrialisation: after it, technology, almost at times for its own sake, swept all before it. The idea became deeply rooted that something done by machinery must be better than anything done by hand, a viewpoint hardly challenged before the closing years of the era.

The 1851 Exhibition was distinguished from those preceding it by its international scope and its resounding success. No other exhibition in the nineteenth century was to be as significant and influential. The decision to make the Exhibition international was taken by Henry Cole and Prince Albert only in 1849, and the two years left for organising it were barely enough. One result of the rushed arrangements was that the printing exhibits were not gathered together in one of the thirty classes into which

47

the Exhibition was divided. Class XVII was devoted to paper and stationery, printing and bookbinding, but printing machinery was in class VI, manufacturing machines; numerous printers were located in class XXX, sculpture, models and plastic art; and foreign printers remained with their individual countries. This rather muddled arrangement prevented the juries, and presumably the visitors, from seeing all the printing exhibits. Nevertheless, a very representative collection of material was exhibited and the requirement that specimens of a new process had to be shown kept out all the impractical inventions.

Two classes of medal were awarded—the Council Medal for originality, and the Prize Medal for excellence in production or workmanship. The only Council Medal awarded for printing went to the Imperial Court and Government Printing Office of Vienna for galvanoplastic (a form of nature printing) and chemitype. The jury would have given one to Thomas de la Rue as well, had he not been one of its members. It is not always clear exactly what Prize Medals were awarded for, but printers were given about seven in class XVII for printing illustrations as well as receiving five Honourable Mentions. In class XXX there were nine Prize Medals and four Honourable Mentions. Most of the awards went to foreign printers.

Among those showing lithography were Hullmandel & Walton (a partnership dating from about 1843), Hanhart, and Day & Son, as the firm of Day & Haghe had by this time become.[1] Anastatic printing was exhibited by Rudolph Appel, who was awarded a Prize Medal, S. H. Cowell and J. & J. Leighton. John Gould showed his method of reproducing the metallic colouring of humming birds, which he used in his books about them. Bradbury & Evans were awarded a Prize Medal, and showed, among other things, wood engravings. Baxter received an Honourable Mention for colour printing, which was also exhibited by J. M. Kronheim and William Dickes. Binns & Goodwin of Bath showed natural illustration. Engraving machines were exhibited by J. Huntley and Charles Chabot, and the latter also showed his method of transfer zincography. G. J. Cox exhibited specimens of his method of transferring copper and steel engravings to lithographic stones. In the French Section Firmin Gillot of Paris displayed his invention of paneiconography, a method of relief etching: the artist drew on a polished zinc plate with lithgraphic ink or crayon; the plate was then rolled up with ink and dusted with finely powdered rosin, which adhered only to the inked image, before being etched with dilute sulphuric or hydrochloric acid to produce a relief metal block.

Books about the Exhibition itself used a number of different illustration processes. The *Official Descriptive and Illustrated Catalogue* was illustrated mainly with wood engravings, but also had some very pleasing tinted lithographs by Day & Son of John Bourne's views of the suspension bridge at Kiev, some monochrome lithographs and chromolithographs—the latter also by Day—and one colour print by F. W. Rowney's typochromatic printing. *Tallis's History and Description of the Crystal Palace*, 1852, had steel engravings copied from daguerreotypes made for John Tallis by Richard Beard and J. E. Mayall.[2] Baxter produced a volume of prints with a short text, *Baxter's Gems of the Great Exhibition*. J. McNevin's *A Souvenir of the Great Exhibition* had six chromolithographed plates by Day & Son at 2 guineas, the plates being described as chromographs and available with additional hand-colouring for 3 guineas.[3] The most impressive book about the Exhibition, however, is perhaps Dickinson Brothers' *Comprehensive Pictures of the Great Exhibition*, completed in two volumes in 1854, which has chromolithographed reproductions, 32·5cm by 49cm, of pictures by Nash, Haghe and Roberts. Another well known book is M. Digby Wyatt's *Industrial Arts of the XIX century*, 1853, which reproduced paintings of various exhibits.

CHROMOLITHOGRAPHY

Chromolithography was probably at the height of its popularity for book illustration in the 1850s, though the number of firms practising it was relatively small. They had to proceed by trial and error, since there does not seem to have been any book of instruction before the 1860s. Fielding's *Art of Engraving*, 1841, has some instructions for making tinted lithographs, though his *Manual of Lithography* (in *The Theory of Painting*, 1842) has not; tinted lithographs are also described in *Everyman His Own Printer*, 1854, published by Waterlow to promote the use of his 'autographic' press. The earliest English printer's handbook to describe chromolithography as such appears to be G. Ruse & C. Straker's *Printing and Its Accessories*, published about 1860; the lithographic parts of it were written by Straker, who published *Instructions in the Art of Lithography* in 1867 in which he included a chapter on the preparation of stones and how to print a chromolithograph. Both books are illustrated with impressions from the individual stones and the complete chromolithograph that resulted. The most comprehensive work to appear in England during the Victorian period on this subject was W. D. Richmond's *The Grammar of Lithography*, 1878, a very successful book that continued to be reprinted until at least 1890. It was translated into German, a rare distinction at a time when German printing and its output of technological literature was in advance of English. Richmond was born in Gloucestershire and took charge of the lithographic printing department at Wyman & Sons in 1874. His book is slightly disappointing in having few illustrations, but it was intended as a cheap practical handbook. G. A. Audsley's *Art of Chromolithography*, 1888, has a very short account of the subject, but shows a print in twenty-two colours with progressive proofs.

Chromolithography was a slow and painstaking method of printing and the books containing illustrations produced in this way were expensive: the *Industrial Arts of the XIX century* cost 17 guineas, and the most famous of Owen Jones's books, *The Grammar of Ornament*, 1856, cost £19 12s. The books illustrated with chromolithographs have been dealt with in detail by a number of writers and will not be considered in detail here. Numerically they were few in proportion to all illustrated books. Because of their expense a great number of them are gift books whose subject matter hardly rises above the trivial, or mock gothic manuscripts. They were for the most part too expensive for all but the rich, and as the century wore on they seem to have declined in numbers. Monochrome lithography remained a moderately popular method of illustration (see Appendix), but few outstanding books were illustrated lithographically.

TRANSFER LITHOGRAPHY

As early as 1819 Senefelder had described in his *Complete Course in Lithography* various methods and styles of transfer lithography —a process by which the lithographer's drawing on paper was transferred by running it through the press face down on the stone. This had the advantage, especially for lettering, that the original did not need to be laterally inverted; so it was particularly useful for jobbing work, billheads and so forth. It is difficult to distinguish a transfer lithograph from one drawn direct on the stone, in the absence of any statement on the plate or in the book.

ANASTATIC PRINTING

There is not a great deal of evidence for the use of transfer lithography in book illustration, except in anastatic printing, a process thought of in its day as a great innovation and now interesting as an example of the Victorians' passion for technological advance.

It was originally intended as a facsimile printing process and was first mentioned in England in an announcement in the *Athenaeum* of December 1841 that the journal was to be reprinted in Berlin anastatically (without its consent). The inventor of the process was said to be M. Baldermus, and it was introduced into England in 1844 by (Sir) William Siemens and patented (No 10,219) in the name of Joseph Woods.[4] The novelty behind it was that the transfer could be made from the page of an old book, the patent specifying that the original must be in ink 'of a saponaceous or fatty nature', which includes linseed oil inks, the most common variety up to that time. The leaf to be reprinted was soaked with dilute nitric acid for a period depending on its age—thirty or forty years required some days' soaking, but the maximum suggested was ten days—then the impression was transferred to a zinc plate by passing print and plate through the rolling press. If the original was very old it was first revived by a preliminary soaking in potash and then a solution of tartaric acid. When the image was inked with a roller, the ink would refuse to take on the white areas, where crystals of bi-tartrate of potash had formed. After reviving the print in this way, the tartrate was washed out and the print treated in the same way as a more recent one to make a lithographic printing plate.

The early accounts of anastatic printing name Baldermus as the inventor, but later in the century the credit for it was claimed by Rudolph Appel. The scanty details of his career that survive, however, tend to suggest that he was not always scrupulously honest. He is said to have been an employee of Baldermus who came to England with Siemens. In a series of letters to Sir Thomas Phillipps Appel once informed him that a special press was needed for anastatic transfer. This was contradicted by a letter from his own printing office later in the same year by saying that any ordinary lithographic press would do. This had been when Phillipps was thinking of doing his own anastatic printing instead of employing Appel. On another occasion he was in partnership with Henry Glynn in patent No 13,717 for the prevention of anastatic forgery. The patent was directed against forgers of cheques and postage stamps, since a number of attempts had been made to forge the latter, although without much success according to Sir Rowland Hill. In order to market the anti-anastatic paper it was necessary, however, for Appel and Glynn to maintain that stamps could be forged anastatically. The stamp printers took exception to this claim and challenged the patentees to produce some anastatically forged stamps. J. B. Bacon of Perkins, Bacon & Petch, the stamp printers, claimed that Appel and Glynn always found some reason for avoiding the challenge. Appel did not make his claim to be the inventor of anastatic printing until after Woods was dead (he died of cholera in 1849) and Siemens was occupied with his successful career in engineering.

Although it is unlikely that Appel can be credited with the invention, its survival in England and exploitation on a minor but persistent scale is largely due to his enthusiasm. The owners of the patent spent 1845 in attempting to perfect a rotary press for large-scale production, and in publicising their process, which was demonstrated at a well reported lecture given to the Royal Institution by Michael Faraday on 25 April.

The first book with anastatic illustrations appears to be *Sketches Printed at the Second Hampstead Conversazione February 2nd, 1846 in Illustration of the Anastatic Printing Process.* The Hampstead Conversaziones were meetings of a scientific and cultural nature, and this particular one was devoted to the now fashionable anastatic printing. Woods sent a press but was not himself present to operate it. The prints were reproduced from originals drawn by members of the audience, among whom was Tenniel, and later bound in buff paper covers and distributed to the members of the conversazione. They were, in fact, examples of the process rather than book illustrations proper.

One of the engineering firms to whom the work of perfecting the press had been given was Ransomes & May of Ipswich. Appel was the manager of the anastatic printing works which had been set up by Siemens some time previously and no doubt visited Ipswich in connection with the work on the press and there met S. H. Cowell. Apparently some anastatic printing was done in 1846, though so far none of it has come to light. In December Siemens and Woods decided to abandon the process and wrote to Appel telling him the works was to be closed.[5] In spite of this, anastatic printing survived through Appel's persistence, and in 1847 and 1848 he was in Ipswich teaching Cowell the process. His name appears on Monson's maps of Ipswich of 1848, 'Printed by Rudolph Appel, Anastatic Printing Office, Ipswich'. In a circular of 1858 Appel mentioned that he had taught Cowell ten years earlier, when, in fact, Cowell had issued a circular announcing that he had added to his business the 'Patent process of Anastatic Printing'. Cowell's earliest anastatic imprint is *Anastatic Sketches for the Portfolio* edited by 'Two Ecclesiologists', published by E. Meadows of Cambridge in parts from 1848 to 1849. From the latter year comes W. J. Hewett's *Twenty Examples . . . from the Misereres of Exeter Cathedral*, published by A. Butler of Shoreham, and from 1850 *Specimens of Ancient Cornish Crosses* by F. C. Hinterton, with the imprint of Parker of Oxford. The printing of plates for publications by provincial publishers was to be, in fact, the principal use of anastatic printing almost to the end of the century.

The first book in England wholly devoted to anastatic printing was Philip de la Motte's *On the Various Applications of Anastatic Printing and Papyrography*, published by David Bogue in 1849. De la Motte's book was itself printed anastatically and it seems likely that he was an amateur rather than a professional printer. He was responsible for the plates in H. E. Strickland & A. G. Melville's *The Dodo and Its Kindred*, 1848, and Sir William Jardine's *Contributions to Ornithology*, 1848. His interest did not last very long and he is better known as a photographer.

One of the results of the display on Appel's stand at the Great Exhibition was probably the work he did for Sir Thomas Phillipps, which was mainly making facsimiles of manuscripts rather than book illustration. It is evident from the correspondence that Appel did not make a very successful living as an anastatic printer, and he eventually went bankrupt in 1857.[6] He sent his customers a circular recommending them to Cowell, whose greater success was no doubt due to his using the process only as part of his printing business. Apart from his work for the Anastatic Drawing Societies (see below) most of Cowell's output comprised antiquarian, topographical and children's books, the last presumably printed in small numbers for circulation among the author's family and friends. An example of this category is *The Giant Show or the Adventures and Misadventures of Benjamin McLummond, Esq.*, 'Printed at the Anastatic Printing Press, Ipswich', and published by Bosworth & Harrison, Regent St, London, and Simkins & Browne, Nottingham.[7] Another, unusual, example is *Story the Xth from Stories of Strange Lands* by Mrs Sarah Lee, a prolific writer of children's books published through

normal commercial channels. Further examples consist of records
of holidays like 'Miss Brown's' *The Foreign Tour of the Misses
Brown, Jones and Robinson at Biarritz and in the Pyrenees,*
evidently inspired by Doyle; and *The Voyage of the 'Amazone'
down the Seine, July 1890,* which is lithographed but clearly in
the anastatic tradition, with a handwritten text reproduced by
transfer.

Antiquarian books with anastatic plates were published before
the Exhibition and continued to be published until the 1890s.
Among the last must be the Rev R. J. Simpson's *Notes and
Sketches of Southrepps Church, Norfolk,* which came out in annual
parts until 1896. A typical example is William Young's *Picturesque Examples of Old English Churches and Cottages from
Sketches in Sussex and Adjoining Counties,* 1869, which was
printed by Cowell and published by S. Birbeck, Belgrave Road,
Birmingham. Cowell published a booklet about 1851, *A Brief
Description of the Art of Anastatic Printing,* in the tenth edition
of which (1881) he listed thirteen archaeological societies for
whom he had printed anastatically.

The Anastatic Drawing Societies were supported by local
antiquaries, for whom they provided a convenient means of
publishing fieldwork. The earlier of them was the Anastatic
Drawing Society, founded in 1854, which issued its first volume
of prints (for 1855) in 1856 under the editorship of the Rev John
M. Gresley. Each member subscribed 10s 6d, for which he
received an annual volume of prints (Plate 16), with a short
text; and members who contributed prints were given ten free
impressions. The Society continued to produce its annual
volumes until 1863, when Gresley ceased to be editor; it did not
restart until 1876, and then ran until 1886. In 1859 another
society, the Ilam Anastatic Drawing Society, had been founded,
and it ran on the same lines as the earlier society until 1873.
The volume for that year was issued in 1875 and in 1876 the two
societies merged and Ilam ceased publication.[8]

Bemrose & Sons of Derby used a similar method of transfer
lithography as anastatic printing. They published a pamphlet

Plate 16   Anastatic print used on a casing. 27·5 × 19·5cm

about it in the late 1860s called *Bemrose and Sons' Process of Fac-simile Printing with Instructions for Using the Instantaneous or Fac-simile Ink*, claiming that their method was superior to anastatic printing, since it could use tracing paper, which anastatic printing could not. It was used in the publications of the Derby Fac-simile Society, which was a very close counterpart to the Anastatic Drawing Societies. The first volume was published in 1866 under the editorship of the Rev C. J. Newdigate of West Hallam, and two more volumes were published in 1869 and 1873. Bemrose claimed that the method was also used for illustrating magazines, but without saying which.

Although anastatic printing lingered on at Cowell's into the 1890s, its days as a useful printing process were clearly numbered. Amateurs could use portable cameras instead of sketchbooks and have the results printed photomechanically if they wished. It was still described in the second edition of the *Account of the Methods and Processes for the Reproduction of Maps of the Ordnance Survey*, published in 1902, but other defunct processes were also left in this edition, their descriptions unchanged from those of 1874. After his bankruptcy Appel was employed at the Ordnance Survey until 1892, which probably accounts for the use of anastatic printing in its original form there. In the volumes of the facsimile *Domesday Book* published at Southampton between 1861 and 1863 there are anastatic facsimiles of wood engravings from the *Illustrated London News* (Plate 17).

The 1850s saw colour printing by relief firmly established, though not so firmly that hand-colouring was entirely ousted. Noel Humphrey's *River Gardens*, 1857, *Ocean Gardens*, 1857, and *The Butterfly Vivarium*, 1858, all had two colours printed and the rest added by hand.[9] All the celebrated colour printers of the second half of the century got into their stride during the 1850s—Edmund Evans, the Vizetellys, G. C. Leighton, Kronheim, Dickes and Fawcett. Some of them had originally been licencees of Baxter, but they generally abandoned his metal key plate towards the end of the decade. Others, such as Evans, never seem to have used this method, making all their blocks from

INTRODUCTION.   vii

part of the original MS. in which he may be more particularly
interested, and whilst the public is gratified by this, Her Majesty's
Government will not be put to the cost of a single shilling for the
production of the work.

HENRY JAMES,

Colonel, Royal Engineers.

Director of the Ordnance Survey, and

Southampton, 31st December, 1863.   Topographical Depôt of the War Office.

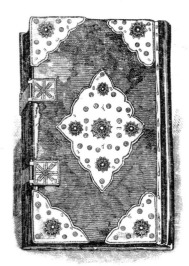
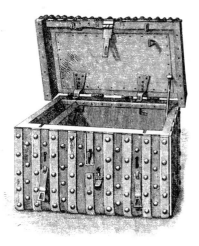

Printed at the Ordnance Survey Office, Southampton.

Plate 17   Anastatic facsimile by Rudolph Appel from *Domesday Book*
(1861–3). 10 × 16·5cm

wood. Although their books are extremely attractive, and represent what was to be the final breakaway from hand-colouring for commercial bookwork, they form only a minute proportion of the illustrated books published at this time.[10]

CHEMITYPE

Chemitype was exhibited at the 1851 Exhibition by the Imperial Printing Office of Vienna, but does not seem to have been used for the illustration of English books at this time. It was invented by a Dane, C. Piil, in 1846 and must have been practised in Denmark as well as Vienna, since it is from the former that the English book illustrations come. They appear in a succession of works published by Williams & Norgate and printed by H. H. Thiele. The author was Professor George Stephens of Copenhagen University, whose best known publication is *The Old Northern Runic Monuments*, which came out in three folio volumes at 50s each in 1866–7, 1867–8 and 1884. Among the others are *Macbeth, Earl Siward and Dundee*, 1876, *Thunor the Thunderer*, 1878, and *Handbook to the Old Northern Runic Monuments*, 1884, an abridgement of the three-volume work that sold at 40s. Stephens' prose style is rather trying and his scholarship was heavily criticised at the time, but his books on runes contain some very attractive illustrations of a subject that is not inherently pictorial (Plate 18).

Chemitype was intended to combine the fineness of line and flexibility of etching with the convenience of being able to print in relief. A zinc plate was used as an etching surface by the artist in the usual way; and as zinc is undercut in the etching process if it is not stopped out, this must have produced a plate with inverted v-shaped lines. Filings of fusible metal were then spread over the plate, which was heated with a spirit lamp that caused the fusible metal to melt and run into all the lines on the etched plate. When cool the metal was planed down until the zinc reappeared and then etched with hydrochloric acid, which attacked the zinc only and eventually left the fusible metal in relief.

Two scribbles, probably by the same hand. The latter has one Old-Northern
letter, the o. From the famous rune-rich Picts-house, long a Wiking rendezvous.

Plate 18   Chemitype. *Handbook to the Old Northern Runic Monuments*
(1884). 9·5 × 18·5cm

NATURE PRINTING

The Imperial Printing Office of Vienna also showed at the Great
Exhibition some interesting intaglio prints of fossilised fish that
had been made by electrotyping casts taken from the originals
with gutta percha—not an ideal material for this purpose. Dr
Ferguson Branson described his own unsuccessful experiments
with this method to the Society of Arts in the year of the Exhibition.[11]

The Imperial Printing office was at this time under the direction of Alois Auer; and its continuing experiments to produce a
satisfactory printing surface from a natural object resulted ultimately in what was to be known in England as nature printing.
Although it was used to illustrate only a few books, it received
considerable publicity and the prints themselves were extra-
ordinarily attractive. The principle used, moreover, was to be
put to use in future printing methods that were commercially
very much more successful. This principle was that an object
placed between two flat surfaces, one harder than the other, and

subjected to pressure will become embedded in the softer one; and a complete intaglio image of the object may be obtained. This principle appears to have been first applied to printing in England in two blocks in the *Journal of Design* for November 1851 illustrating lace patterns, by William Taylor of Nottingham. These illustrations are embossed in white on a blue background, and were made by placing a piece of lace between two boxwood blocks, one of which had been softened by steaming, and pressing them together until the lace was embedded in the softer block, which after its removal could be used as a printing surface. The surface of the block was inked and the pressure of printing produced the embossed effect where the paper was forced into the uninked intaglio portions of the block. The patterns were used to make up books of sample patterns for travellers. Some manufacturers used pattern books in which the embossed effect had not been obtained.

Some of the pattern books showing the embossed effect were sent to Vienna by the Austrian consul in London, and Auer set his men to work to see if they could reproduce lace patterns for printing. They were trying to use gutta percha, without much success, when an overseer named Worring suggested taking the impressions in lead. This was very successful and the idea was extended to plants, the impression being made between a sheet of lead and one of steel. The remains of the plant had to be very carefully removed, the small pieces sometimes requiring a blow-pipe to extract them from the lead. The impression was electrotyped, and from the relief thus obtained an intaglio electrotype was made, and that formed the actual printing plate.

Auer published a book about the process in 1853, *Die Entdeckung des Naturselbstdruckes*. An edition with parallel texts in other languages, which appeared in 1854, has a number of nature prints as illustrations, including lace, a fossil fish, a bat's wing, and various plants. This is the most attractive of Auer's nature printed books, since most of his output in this field consisted of cumbrous folios with plates in sepia, awkward to handle because of their size and tedious to look at.

In 1852 Henry Bradbury, the son of William Bradbury of Bradbury & Evans, spent some months in the Imperial Printing Office, where he was shown all the printing methods. He returned home in 1853 and in that year Bradbury & Evans took out patent No 1164 for a method of nature printing very similar to Auer's. Although Auer had patented his method, he claimed that he did not enforce the patent, and he was furious when he learned what had happened. Early in 1854 he published a book denouncing Bradbury. It was printed in four languages, the English title being *Conduct of a Young Englishman Named Henry Bradbury . . . Concerning the Natural-Printing Process.* Bradbury defended himself before the Royal Institution in May 1855 in a lecture whose text was published as a pamphlet in 1856 under the title *Nature-Printing, Its Origin and Objects*—and an edition in German was published at the same time.

He also had started to publicise the new process by issuing in 1854 a folder of plates called *A Few Leaves Represented by 'Nature Printing'*, in which the plates all represent plants and were printed in full colour. Bradbury's method of inking his plates was to apply the darkest colour first in the appropriate area, wipe the plate and then apply successively lighter colours one by one. The embossed appearance typical of nature prints was obtained by using extra thicknesses of blanket on the rolling press. The first book for which he printed the plates was Thomas Moore's *Ferns of Great Britain and Ireland*, published in parts from 1855 to 1856, each part costing 6s and the complete volume 6 guineas. It was another very large book with plates over 54cm tall.

Bradbury's principal achievement in nature printing is to be found in the next two works that Bradbury & Evans published— W. Johnstone & A. Croall's *Nature-printed British Seaweeds* and *The Octavo Nature-printed British Ferns* (Plate 19), the former in four volumes and the latter in two, both published during 1859 and 1860. These are smaller and brighter books than the monumental volumes that had hitherto seemed appropriate for nature printing, and they gain immeasurably from it. They were

Plate XVII

A

B

POLYSTICHUM ACULEATUM, VARS. **A.** LOBATUM, **B.** ARGUTUM.

Nature Printed by Henry Bradbury

Plate 19   Nature print by Henry Bradbury. *The Octavo Nature-printed British Ferns* (1860). 21 × 13cm

given attractive bindings and had decorative title-pages designed by John Leighton. They were relatively expensive at 42s a volume, but no more so than other books on similar subjects.[12] A programme of further volumes with nature-printed plates brought to an end when Bradbury killed himself in 1860. The firm nevertheless exhibited the process at the International Exhibition in 1862 and were awarded a medal.

There are in existence a number of single volumes printed by amateurs who obviously used the original plant as a printing surface. An advertisement leaf in the John Johnson collection describes the Foliographic Press, manufactured by G. J. Cox of Regent Street, London, and selling at 5s 6d, or, large, at 8s 6d. This was a press designed to allow amateurs to print from leaves, though that could be done without any elaborate apparatus, as was demonstrated by F. O. Hutchinson in his *Ferns of Sidmouth*, Sidmouth, 1862, who simply inked the ferns and used the impressions for lithographic transfer.

The idea of making natural impressions remained popular during the second half of the century, and between 1857 and 1883 eleven patents relating to printing in this way were taken out. With one exception, however, they do not seem to have been used. The exception was *The Dictionary of Needlework* by S. F. A. Caulfield & B. C. Saward, issued in parts in 1881–2, in which lace was used to make the impressions for a number of quite spectacular plates, all heavily embossed and for the most part showing the lace in white on a coloured background.

As late as 1895 Edward M. White was advocating in the *Process Photogram* a method of nature printing by exposing the dried skeleton of a plant over a photographic negative, a process that had been used over fifty years earlier by Mrs Anna Atkins in *Photographs of British Algae*.

NATURAL ILLUSTRATION

It is remarkable that, during a century in which more illustrative processes were invented and exploited than ever before in the history of printing, there should have survived a series of examples from the beginning to the end of the century of botanical, and other, books with illustrative specimens stuck in. This form of illustration was represented at the Great Exhibition by Binns & Goodwin of Bath. An earlier, and very spectacular, example was George Sinclair's *Hortus Gramineus Woburnensis*, 1815, which described the experiments undertaken at Woburn at the direction of the Duke of Bedford (who had the work privately published). It was a folio in which all the grasses described were illustrated with dried and coloured specimens.

Binns & Goodwin were using this method in the 1840s, partly for botanical works and partly for drawing-room books. In the latter class were *Wildflowers and Their Teachings*, 1846, and *Ocean Flowers and Their Teachings*, 1847, each containing dried specimens, literary extracts and poems, offered at 15s each. More serious works are represented by Frederick Hanham's *Natural Illustrations of the British Grasses*, 1846 (Plate 20), described in an advertisement as being 'illustrated with 62 Real Specimens carefully preserved and mounted forming a splendid volume in small folio suitable for the library of the Connoisseur, the Study of the Agriculturalist, and the Drawing Room table of the affluent, Price £2.2'. The great drawback of this method of illustration is also mentioned in the advertisement, namely the immense labour involved, 'each 100 copies of the *British Grasses*, for instance, requiring the collection, preparation and mounting of 6,200 distinct specimens'. The results rarely justified the effort, since the plants were difficult to fix securely into the books, were often fragile, and prevented the book from closing properly even when they were guarded in. *The Ferns of Wales* by Edward Young was published in Neath in 1856 and has, oddly enough, a lithographed title-page, quite nicely printed in two tints by Schenk & McFarlane of Edinburgh from a photograph of the Vale of Neath. It is surprising that lithography was not also used for the plates (Plate 21).

An example from the end of the century is F. M. Halford's *Dry Fly Entomology, a Brief Description of Leading Types of Natural Insects Serving as Food for Trout and Grayling*, 1897,

MILIUM EFFUSUM.—Spreading Millet Grass,

Plate 20 Natural illustration from F. Hanham's *The British Grasses* (1846). 29 × 18cm

whose second volume consists of 100 specimens of flies arranged in sunken mounts. Books on textiles are often illustrated in this way: Antonio Sansone in 1888 published *Dyeing*, illustrated with inserted specimens of cloth, and a supplement, *Recent Progress in the Industries of Dyeing and Calico Printing*, 3 volumes, 1895-7, with over 400 inserted samples.

GLYPHOGRAPHY

Another process shown by the Imperial Printing Office of Vienna was glyphography, described in the *Reports by the Juries* under the name of galvanoglyphy; it was used in England to illustrate a few dozen books between 1842 and 1873, and certain Continental printing offices besides that of Vienna also used it. It was invented by Edward Palmer, who developed it from an earlier process called electrotint, a method of making relief plates by electrotyping. Glyphographs were made on a metal plate stained black, over which was spread an opaque white composition. The artist drew on the plate with a variety of pointed instruments that removed the composition as he drew, enabling him to see the black plate underneath and thus judge the progress of his drawing. When the plate was finished, it was heightened by the application of additional material where the composition remained on the surface, and finally electrotyped—thus a relief printing block could be obtained. Palmer patented glyphography (No 9227) in 1842 and in the same year published a pamphlet about it, *Glyphography; or, Engraved Drawings*, which contains a number of examples of the process and some instruction in how to work it. It was used commercially in John Lindley's *The Vegetable Kingdom*, 1846 (and in the second and third editions, 1847 and 1851). The most notable artist to use it was George Cruikshank, for it appeared in seven of his books, including *The Bottle*, 1847, and *The Drunkard's Children*, 1848. It is surprising that a method that could produce the appearance of a wood engraving without an engraver needing to intervene between the artist and the print should not have been more widely used.[13]

Plate 21 Tinted lithographic title page to E. Young's *The Ferns of Wales* (1856). Original in black and two colours with traces of hand colouring. 31 × 20cm

Chapter Four

WOOD ENGRAVING
1850-1900

THE 'SIXTIES' SCHOOL

IN THE second half of the century two styles of wood engraving are discernible—the old vignette and a new style based on painting and pen and ink drawing. The latter was often alarmingly divorced from any consideration of illustration as part of book design, an unfortunate development associated principally with what is known in the history of book illustration as 'The Sixties'. This is a convenient label attached to work done, mainly between 1855 and 1875, by a number of Victorian artists in illustrating imaginative literature. Most of them owed their reputations to their work as narrative painters, and they produced narrative paintings and drawings that were reproduced by wood engraving and inserted into books. The originator of this style is generally considered to be Sir John Gilbert, whose most famous work was his *Shakespeare*, issued in parts from 1856 to 1858.[1] Because their work has been much studied, these artists have tended to overshadow the period. There is no reason, however, why book illustration should be regarded as the prerogative of imaginative literature. If it can be said that 'an illustrated book is a partnership between author and artist to which the artist contributes something which is a pictorial comment on the author's words or an interpretation of his meaning in another medium',[2] then this applies to factual as well as imaginative work, and to illustrators other than artists.

The fame of the 'Sixties' illustrators originates in Gleeson White's *English Illustrators, the Sixties,* written about 1896. At that time the artists extolled in it were still enjoying a level of esteem which was destined to plummet. Leighton, Fildes and Fred Walker, to take a few examples, are no longer considered outstanding European artists, and even Millais, who has lasted better than most, only really survives in his pre-Raphaelite phase.[3] A better writer on the subject than White was Forrest Reid, whose *Illustrators of the Sixties* was published in 1928. Reid regards William Allingham's *Music Master,* 1855, illustrated by Arthur Hughes and D. G. Rossetti, as the first 'Sixties' book; but although it contains one illustration that is now highly thought of, 'The Maids of Elfen-Mere', he considers it disappointing. Probably the most famous 'Sixties' book is Tennyson's *Poems,* published by Moxon in 1857, and containing fifty-five illustrations—thirty by Millais, Holman Hunt and Rossetti, the remainder by such academic artists as Mulready, Maclise and Landseer. Though famous, it is an unsatisfactory book, for the illustrations do not go well together, and, for this reason, it was a failure in its day—the pre-Raphaelites' admirers objected to the conventional illustrations almost as much as the supporters of the conventional artists objected to the pre-Raphaelites. It cannot be said that the latter are particularly successful, though the book's reputation rests on them, since they are pictures rather than illustrations, for the most part printed inside frames that successfully divorce them from the text. In some cases they have little to do with the poems they supposedly illustrate: Millais produced one illustration, 'The Death of the Old Year', so startlingly irrelevant that Reid thought it must have been intended for 'The Owl', a poem that does not appear in the text at all; and D. G. Rossetti's 'St Cecilia' is so remote from the poem that no one from Tennyson on has been able to see its relevance.

A large proportion of these 'Sixties' illustrations were printed in periodicals rather than books. Associated with their rather inflated reputation is that of the brothers George and Edward Dalziel, as the only important firm of wood engravers in the latter part of the century. Their reputation rests on their book, *The Brothers Dalziel*, published in 1901, most of which is taken up with their relationship to artists, particularly with letters of congratulation on the excellence of their work. That this was not the universal view of their clients can be seen from Rossetti's comments:

> These engravers! What ministers of wrath! Your drawing comes to them like Agag, delicately, and is hewn in pieces before the Lord Harry. I took more pains with one block lately than I had done with anything for a long while. It came back to me on paper, the other day, with Dalziel performing his cannibal jig in the corner, and I have really felt like an invalid ever since. As yet I fare best with W. J. Linton. He keeps stomach aches for you, but Dalziel deals in fevers and agues.
>
> *Address to Dalziel Brothers*
>
> O woodman spare that block,
>   O gash not anyhow!
> It took ten days by clock,
>   I'd fain protect it now.
>
> *Chorus*—Wild laughter from Dalziels' Workshop.[4]

On the whole their book is disappointing, supplying few details on the running of their business, and occasionally it is misleading, giving the impression, for example, that the firm was responsible for all the blocks in Moxon's Tennyson, though actually they cut only fifteen. The Dalziels were competent and well-organised engravers, but only one firm out of many. In 1872 there were 128 firms of wood engravers listed in the *Post Office Directory* at work in London. W. J. Linton probably made better blocks than the Dalziels, and he was also the author of several books on the subject that are more illuminating than theirs, which seems to have been written largely to boost their own reputation. The jury at the International Exhibition of 1862 awarded only two medals for wood engraving, one of them to Linton (the Dalziels did not exhibit).

A balanced view of the activities of the wood engravers can best be obtained perhaps from the illustrated advertisements that appeared in the *Publishers' Circular* during the 1850s, 1860s and 1870s, and which offer an interesting synopsis of what was going into books. Engravings proliferate, good, bad and indifferent, but by no means dominated by the Dalziels. The majority are not signed at all, as was general among wood engravers throughout the century. Much excellent and attractive work was done anonymously and within the confines of good book design, though the weaknesses of typography at this time rarely allow justice to be done to the illustrations. Plenty of factual books were well illustrated. Samuel Smiles' *Lives of the Engineers . . . George and Robert Stephenson*, 1879, is full of engravings in the vignette tradition that add considerably to the reader's appreciation of the text; they are placed with the relevant letterpress, and are generally small and unpretentious. The book would be the poorer without them. In the field of imaginative interpretation of fact Doré's illustrations to Jerrold's *London*, 1872, are outstanding, with their perspective of misty sunshine in 'The Ladies Mile', and gloom, darkness and degradation in 'Dudley Street, Seven Dials' and 'Under the Arches'.

It is difficult to define exactly what is meant by a 'Sixties' book,[5] but it seems to be one that is imaginative, in verse or prose, with illustrations by a Victorian artist reproduced by competent if often unexciting wood engraving. The great exceptions are Tenniel's illustrations to the *Alice* books, where the text and illustrations harmonise remarkably well for their period. It is perhaps significant that these are the only noteworthy illustrations Tenniel ever made. One other notable book with wood-engraved illustrations that have been fitted into the text is *The Water Babies*, 1885, with illustrations by Linley Sambourne.

This has been called 'the only distinguished woodcut book of the 'eighties'.[6]

PRINTING PRESSES AND WOOD BLOCKS

Various technical improvements affected the printing of wood engravings in the second half of the century, and one of these was the design of printing presses. The Napier and Hopkinson & Cope power platen presses were available by the 1840s. Efficient cylinder presses were also on the market and their design continued to be improved throughout the century. It is difficult to decide what sort of press a book was printed on simply by looking at it,[7] but there is some evidence that the hand press was generally abandoned for most bookwork around the middle of the century. Edmund Evans is said to have printed his last book on a hand press, *A Chronicle of England*,[8] in 1864. Moxon's Tennyson was printed on a hand press in 1857, which was sufficiently unusual apparently to be recorded by the Dalziels, who were not much interested in technical matters in their book.

The degree of skill called for from the engraver varied according to the way in which the artist prepared the block. Two styles of engraving for reproduction were described by T. H. Fielding in his *Art of Engraving*, 1841: one he called the 'laid on' style, in which the artist used Indian ink to lay on his main tints and then finished the drawing with a pencil; and the second, which he considered required less skill, was the 'facsimile' style, in which the artist drew on the block every line the engraver was to cut.

Box is a small tree and the diameter of the trunk did not admit the manufacture of end grain blocks of any great size; so if the illustration was over 5in square, it had to be engraved on a composite block made from two or more pieces of box glued together. Various methods of bolting them were devised from time to time, but the only real advantage of this was to enable several engravers to work on the same illustration simultaneously. This practice speeded up the making of a block, but it is unlikely that the practice occurred outside periodical publication.

ELECTROTYPING

In 1841 Fielding wrote: 'We have no doubt that in a very short time stereotyping woodcuts will be entirely superseded by the voltaic process', by which he meant electrotyping, which had been discovered in 1839. His surmise appears to have been substantially correct, though when exactly stereotyping was abandoned for illustration purposes, if at all, it is difficult to say. J. Southward wrote as late as 1882:[9] 'Electrotyping has almost superseded stereotyping in reproducing wood engravings'. Two years later J. S. Hodson stated: 'Stereotyping, however useful for type work and for ordinary printing, is quite out of the question for art work, as notwithstanding all the modern improvements the results are too chancy for anything requiring sharpness and delicacy in the results.'[10]

Electrotyping as a practicable method of manufacturing facsimiles was discovered by Thomas Spencer of Liverpool, and

Plate 22   The first electrotype illustration, from the *London Journal of Arts and Sciences* (1840). 7 × 17cm. Reproduced by courtesy of the Curators of the Bodleian Library

others all working independently, about 1839. Spencer suggested two methods by which it might be used for copying wood engravings, in a book he published in 1840 called *Instructions for the Multiplication of Works of Art by Voltaic Electricity*: one was to impress the block into soft lead which was then used as the cathode; and the other was to deposit a metallic face on the block and make first a mould and then an electrotype from that. His first idea was the right one and it quickly went into use, though using gutta percha or wax to make the mould instead of lead.[11] The first electrotype illustration published in England was sent to the *London Journal of Arts and Sciences* in April 1840 by Alfred Smee (Plate 22), though oddly enough it is a reproduction of an intaglio plate. A fairly early use of electrotype for making intaglio plates was J. Thompson's *The Seasons*, published by Longman in 1842, with illustrations by members of the Etching Club. Robert Branston was an early worker at electrotyping and made a specimen for William Savage's *Dictionary of the Art of Printing*, published in 1841. Warren de la Rue was also working in the same field, and was successfully making electrotypes from wood engravings by 1843.

Savage explained how electrotyping worked in his *Dictionary* thus:

> This is effected by placing the object to be copied in a solution of any metal, when the galvanic action precipitates the metal from the liquid that held it in solution, upon the engraving that is to be copied. This precipitation or deposition assumes the form of a cake of pure metal, with every line, however delicate, and every inequality, however minute, on its surface, so as to form a matrix or mould in the highest state of perfection.

One of the factors that made electrotyping practicable was the steady current available from the Daniell cell, although this was replaced fairly soon in England by Smee's cell as the most popular power source with electrotypers. In 1878 the firm of Dellagana of Shoe Lane installed a dynamo, an innovation quickly adopted by others as it reduced the period of deposition by three-quarters, though it was found that the quality of the electrotype was adversely affected and fewer impressions could be obtained from dynamo than cell electros. It is likely that by the second half of the century many, if not most, wood engravings used in bookwork were printed from electrotypes. This, at least, was the practice recommended by contemporary writers on the printing of illustrations, mainly to avoid the danger of the block breaking.[12]

PHOTOGRAPHY AND WOOD ENGRAVING

Photography was applied to wood engraving from the first, though its impact did not begin to be felt for another twenty years. It involved photographing an artist's drawing and printing it on the surface of a block as a guide to the engraver, which was first accomplished in blocks that appeared in the *Magazine of Science* on 27 April 1839 (Plate 23) and *The Mirror* on 20 April. The former magazine had been carrying a series of articles on photography, and the person responsible for the not very inspired illustrations was G. Francis. They were followed up on 4 May by two more blocks, of Erith church, obviously made from wood engravings that had been made transparent. The directions for preparing a block were to soak its face in a solution of 20 grains of salt in 1oz of water for five minutes, then dry it and soak it again in a solution of 60 grains of silver nitrate to 1oz of water. This would cause the formation of silver chloride on the surface of the block, making it light sensitive. No instructions about exposure were offered. The soaking must have damaged the surface of the block, and it is likely that the process was considerably more difficult than the instructions in the magazine made out.

Although some engravers used photography to fix drawings on their blocks, they tended to keep the precise method of manipulation to themselves. A number of engravers were working on the problem during the early 1850s, and the first to achieve much success appears to have been Robert Langton, an example of whose work was published in the *Art-Journal* in 1854. An accompanying letter from the Rev St Vincent Beechey claims that the image was transferred on to the block by photog-

THE

MAGAZINE OF SCIENCE,

And School of Arts.

| No. IV.] | SATURDAY, APRIL 27, 1839. | [Price 1½d. |

FAC-SIMILES OF PHOTOGENIC DRAWINGS.

THIRD EDITION

Plate 23 Wood engraving from a photograph on the block (1839).
15 × 12·5cm. Reproduced by courtesy of the Curators of the Bodleian
Library

raphy. Langton said he had been experimenting for four years before being able to produce anything satisfactory, and exhibited his print, a photograph of the moon, at the Caxton Exhibition in 1877 with a claim that it was 'the earliest invention of photographing on wood'.

The Dalziels have left a record of how they proceeded: 'After spending much time and labour in experimenting, as well as spoiling a great many blocks, we succeeded in getting fairly good photographs for the engraver's purpose on other pieces of wood, and so the valuable original drawings were preserved.'

Traditionally the first book published with photographic wood engravings is Catherine Winkworth's *Lyra Germanica*, 1861, in which the illustration was printed on the block and engraved by Thomas Bolton from a negative taken by John Leighton of Flaxman's relief 'Deliver Us from Evil'. It is mentioned in the section added by Bohn to Jackson's *Treatise on Wood Engraving* when he brought it up to date in 1861; he gave no details of how it was done, but there are a number of other accounts.

Carl Hentschel in a paper on process engraving he read to the Society of Arts in 1900 dated the introduction of photography on the block to about 1868, and described how he had helped his father to carry it out. It was kept secret until John Swain adopted it, though whether he was given the secret or discovered the same method for himself is not clear. The reason for the secrecy was that the manipulation was regarded as too simple to patent. The elder Hentschel's method was very effective: an albumen silver print was pasted face downwards on the block with 'some special glue of his own', and when it was dry the paper backing was rubbed away with a moistened finger, leaving the image laterally inverted on the block. When it was cut, it would print the right way round. The great advantage of this procedure was that it minimised the amount of moisture that had to be applied to the surface of the block. C. T. Jacobi in the *Printers' Handbook*, 1905, said that there were several methods of photographing on to the block, though he did not seem to know about Hentschel's. They all had the object of covering the block with a thin film and preventing moisture from sinking into the surface. He recommended an albumen solution sensitised with silver nitrate painted on the surface of the block and dried in darkness and warmth. A negative was exposed on to it and the print fixed with hypo.

The only book devoted to the subject was written by E. Y. Grupe, an American wood engraver of Burlington, Iowa, and called *Instruction in the Art of Photographing on Wood*, 1882. He described the albumen method, using as a sensitising agent nitrate of silver and collodion. He thought that photography on the block had been in use in America for only a few years before he wrote his book and that it had made a noticeable difference to wood engraving. Another American writer on the subject was Thomas W. Smillie, who is unusual in being preoccupied with scientific rather than artistic wood engraving.[13] He dated the application of photography to his craft to about 1868, and remarked on the difficulty of obtaining accurate scientific reproductions when the original drawing had to be interpreted by a copyist. He had first used a carbon transfer, which gave a good image but led to difficulties owing to the thickness of the film. He had also used the albumen silver method, which made the wood pithy, and bromo-gelatine, but that needed a lot of washing, which made large blocks swell and crack. He finally settled on a system very like Hentschel's, developing the film with very short exposures, transferring it to the block by pressure and stripping off the paper backing. He used this method at the Smithsonian Institution in Washington, DC, from 1869 until photo-mechanical methods came into use.

From the little evidence we have, it seems that photography on the block came into use in England in the 1860s. It benefited the artists, who were often able to sell the original drawing, which was not destroyed, and thus obtain an additional fee,[14] but wood engravers were not so enthusiastic. Linton, writing in 1884, accepted that the method had come to stay, but said it was unpleasant for the engraver, who often had the original beside him and suffered from eyestrain from having to look from the

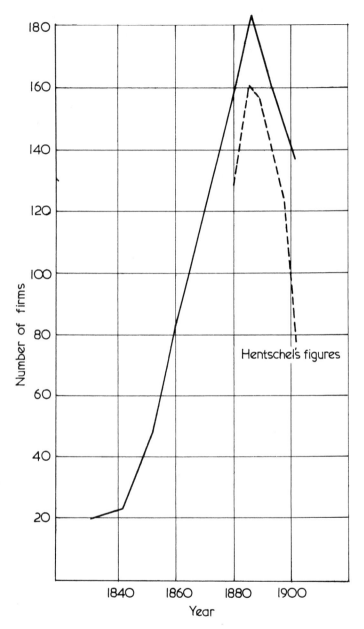

Fig 1 Firms of wood engravers listed in the London directories

block to the original and back many times. By 1896 Kelly's *Post Office Directory* was listing 'Photographers on wood' as a separate trade. There were six firms listed at this time, which had declined to five by 1900. It is probably significant that they were all in the Fleet Street area and doubtless worked predominantly for newspapers and periodicals.

The progress of wood engraving can be seen quite clearly from the number of firms at work in Fig 1. One set of figures is taken from the directories, which were never particularly accurate, but, since the interest of the diagram is in the relative numbers, this is not unduly important. It is possible that the second set of figures, which are those given by Carl Hentschel in his lecture to the Society of Arts, are more accurate, since he would know which firms actually did the work. The directories listed all those who claimed they could carry out wood engraving, perhaps without necessarily doing the work themselves. In both cases there is a steep rise to the mid-1880s, followed by an almost equally steep fall. Until the 1880s wood engraving was probably the commonest method of illustrating books, from the cheapest works—penny novels were illustrated with wood in the 1840s—to relatively expensive gift books. Its use culminated in the exclusive Kelmscott Press publications of the 1890s.

Chapter Five

THE SIXTIES—
THE IMPACT OF
PHOTOGRAPHY

THE FIRST person to make permanently fixed images with a camera was Joseph Nicephore Niepce (1765–1833), who spent most of his life at Saint-Loup-de-Varennes, a small village 4 miles south of Châlons-sur-Saône. It was already known that bitumen of Judea bleached slightly when exposed to light but Niepce discovered that it also hardened and would form an acid resist. Using zinc as a base and an engraving made translucent as an original, he made some prints by placing the original directly on the zinc, which had been coated with light-sensitive material. The resulting heliograph was etched and Niepce was able to make several prints of an engraving of Cardinal d'Amboise in 1827.

Louis Daguerre (1787–1851), working in Paris, succeeded in fixing reversed images on metal by 1839. His pictures were very successful, though impracticable for book illustration, being printed on metal. It should have been possible to etch these plates and use them as printing surfaces, but this proved extremely difficult and only a very few books were illustrated in this way on the continent. In England the only influence that daguerreotypes had on book illustration was as originals for wood engravings, and they were used in this way in Henry Mayhew's *London Labour and the London Poor*, 1851, though one would not know if the captions did not say so. The first book about photography published in London was either a little eight-page instruction book produced by Ackermann and called *Photogenic Drawing Apparatus*, which accompanied a box of materials for making prints by superposition, or N. Whittock's *Photogenic drawing made easy*. Both appeared in 1839.

CALOTYPES

W. H. Fox Talbot (1800–77) was a gentleman of independent means who lived on his estate at Lacock Abbey in Wiltshire and experimented with photography during the 1830s. He succeeded in producing negatives from which an unlimited number of positive copies could be printed about the same time as Daguerre, and patented his process in 1841. He called the prints calotypes. They were far less popular during the 1840s than daguerreotypes, particularly as Talbot demanded hefty licence fees from those who wished to make them. Although he wanted complete control over photography in England, Talbot wanted also to popularise the process, and in order to produce a large number of prints set up a printing establishment at Reading under the charge of his former valet, Nikolaas Henneman. From there he supplied photographic materials to amateurs as well as selling finished calotypes, and it was at Reading that the first calotypes used for book illustration were made. There is some evidence that the first book to be illustrated in this way was a memorial to Catherine, the daughter of John Walter II, proprietor of *The Times*: she died in January 1844, and a booklet called the *Record of C.M.W.* was privately printed and distributed to friends of the family, probably in the spring of that year. Henneman made a calotype of a bust of Catherine Walter, which appeared as a frontispiece, the prints being pasted in after the book was bound and pressed with a hot iron to smooth and dry them.[1]

Record of C.M.W., however, was not published commercially and so hardly dislodges Fox Talbot's own *The Pencil of Nature* from its position as the first published book illustrated photographically. The first of its six parts was published on 29 June 1844, with five pasted in calotypes, and the remaining parts had from three to seven prints each. Part 2 came out in January 1845, and all six parts had been published by April 1846. The introduction to part 1 contains Talbot's account of the history of his invention. Since the primary object of the book was to publicise calotype rather than illustrate a text, *The Pencil of Nature* is a rather dubious example of book illustration. Talbot's next book, *Sun Pictures in Scotland*, 1845, has no text at all. It is likely that both books were published in very small editions.[2] The Reading establishment closed in 1847.

Although no books illustrated with calotypes were shown at the Great Exhibition, 130 special copies of the *Reports by the Juries* were illustrated with calotypes, each copy containing 155 prints. Henneman was occupied from September to November 1851 in making them.

In spite of Fox Talbot's belief that photography in England came under the control of his patent, a certain amount of progress was made. Glass superseded paper for negatives in 1848, and F. S. Archer invented the wet collodion process in 1851. One major event in the advance of photography in this country was the injunction issued by Talbot against Silvester Laroche in 1853, and the latter's refusal to accept it. The case went for trial in 1854. Talbot lost, and the public feeling against his attitude towards photography prevented him from continuing to obstruct its progress.[3] As a result books illustrated with pasted-in photographs became more numerous in the 1850s, and reached the height of their popularity in the 1860s, after which there was a slow but steady decline (see Appendix).

PHOTOGRAPHS AS BOOK ILLUSTRATIONS

One of the most significant things about these books was the variety of subjects which they illustrated and the very ordinary nature of most of them. They were intended to bring illustration to ordinary readers and most of them were moderately priced as illustrated books go. The topographical books produced by Frith and others provided the first accurate book illustration of countries too distant for the majority of Englishmen to visit. Francis Frith went to Egypt in 1856 and 1857 and, in the face of infinite difficulties, took photographs of numerous antiquities, which were published by Virtue in 1858-9 in *Egypt and Palestine, Photographed and Described by Francis Frith* and other books. Frith made three journeys altogether and his photographs were used in the illustration of seven books.[4] He also published some books of English scenery, one of which, *The Gossiping Photographer at Hastings*, 1864, priced at 21s, has a composite photographic title-page showing a view and two portraits of the author.

A number of books appeared about the Far East: Captain Melville Clarke's *From Simla through Ladac and Cashmere* had thirty-seven photographs, and John Thomson's *Antiquities of Cambodia*, published in 1867, had sixteen large photographs. Topographical books about Europe were also popular. F. G. Stephens published *Normandy, its Gothic Architecture and History* in 1865 with twenty-five photographic illustrations of high quality for 25s. Photographs were now more than just a novelty. In 1862 the preface to William & Mary Howitt's *Ruined Abbeys and Castles of Great Britain* claimed: 'In this volume the Publisher has availed himself of the accuracy of photography to present to the reader the precise aspect of the places which, at the same time, are commended to his notice by the pen. . . . The reader is no longer left to suppose himself at the mercy of the imaginations, the caprices, or the deficiencies of artists, but to have the genuine presentment of the object under consideration' (Plate 24).

Photographs made ideal souvenirs and some books were obviously aimed at this market. Queen Victoria's passion for Scotland made it fashionable for tourists, and publishers capitalised on the fact. Some examples have two publishers' names in

TINTERN ABBEY.   83

to narrow rims of ftone, ftill preferve their original form.
The weftern window, with its rich tracery, is extremely
beautiful. " From the length of the nave," fays Coxe, " the
height of the walls, the afpiring form of the pointed arches,
and the fize of the eaft window which clofes the perfpective,
the firft impreffions are thofe of grandeur and fublimity.   But
as thefe emotions fubfide, and we defcend from the contempla-

WEST DOOR AND WINDOW.

tion of the whole to the examination of the parts, we are no
lefs ftruck with the regularity of the plan, the lightnefs of the
architecture, and the delicacy of the ornaments.   We feel
that elegance is its characteriftic no lefs than grandeur, and

Plate 24 Pasted-in photograph from W. & M. Howitt's *Ruined
Abbeys and Castles of Great Britain* (1862). 7·5 × 7cm

their imprint, like W. J. Pringle's *Melrose Abbey in Twelve Photographic Views*, published by Marion & Co in London and Carlisle, and Webb of Edinburgh in 1870; the prints are pasted on to rectos (right-hand pages) and are mainly about 17cm by 16cm, while the captions (they are too short to be called text) are on the facing versos. An edition of Scott's *Marmion* published by A. W. Bennett in 1866 is illustrated with small photographs by Thomas Annan quite nicely inserted, with captions in blue-grey ink, and is bound in varnished boards 'made of wood grown on Flodden Field' with transfer engravings on front and back.

One particularly successful subject for photographically illustrated books was art.[5] In 1860 R. H. Smith wrote his *Expositions of the Cartoons of Raphael*, which was illustrated with photographs printed by Negretti & Zambra, and it went into a second edition in 1861. In his introduction Smith claimed that the book's publication had caused the pictures to be moved out of a dark gallery into the light. Evidently there was a need for a book on the subject since he felt it necessary to inform his readers that Raphael was not a pre-Raphaelite. F. W. Maynard, the secretary of the Arundel Society, published two volumes of reproductions of the publications of the society containing large numbers of photographs reduced to one-fifth of the size of the originals. The first volume, *Descriptive Notice of the Drawings and Publications of the Arundel Society from 1849 to 1868*, 1869, has 205 photographs. The object of the society was 'promoting the knowledge of art', and membership cost a guinea a year, in return for which the society issued chromolithographs, engravings and books of illustrations. The second volume took the record up to 1873.

Even provincial publishers used photographs for illustration. For instance, T. L. Pridham's *Devonshire Worthies*, 1869, published by Henry S. Eland of Exeter, has a number of plates, mostly of statues and engravings but occasionally from life.

One of the difficulties facing photographers in the mid-nineteenth century was the tendency of their prints to fade, which was caused by insufficient washing after development. The washing agent was hyposulphite of soda, a fairly expensive chemical—6s per pound according to Harrison's *History of Photography*, 1888. One attempt to overcome this fading, whose cause was imperfectly understood, was to tone the prints with chloride of gold, which generally gave them a not unpleasing purplish-brown colour. Other disadvantages of using photographs for book illustration was that the cost of the prints did not decrease as the number required increased, and that the rate of production was slow, about six prints a day originally.[6] This slow rate of production doubtless accounts for the absence of photographs as illustrations in periodicals.

Occasionally photographs were used in conjunction with other methods. *Shakespeare's Household Words*, published by Griffiths & Farran about 1859, has a photograph pasted into the centre of a chromolithographed frontispiece. The Howitts' *Ruined Abbeys* has photographs incorporated into the casing.

Photographs were also used as originals for other methods of illustration, as daguerreotypes had been. As late as 1888 the engraved frontispiece of Sir William Siemens in Poole's *Life of Siemens* is captioned 'engraved from a photograph taken by Mr Van der Weyde, with the electric light in 1880'. Another example is J. B. Waring's *Masterpieces of Industrial Art and Sculpture at the International Exhibition, 1862*, published in three folio volumes by Day & Son in 1863, and illustrating about 1,000 objects in 300 plates. Waring claimed that it was the most important work ever executed in chromolithography, using nearly 3,000 litho stones and 40 tons of paper. The lithographs were supervised by Albert Warren and G. MacCulloch, the objects selected having been photographed and then coloured by hand under the direction of W. R. Tymms. It was only the size of Day's establishment that enabled the book to be produced so quickly, and it must have been clear that the cumbersome methods of production were far from ideal. One obvious way of speeding things up was to photograph directly on to the stones instead of copying the photographs by hand, and, in fact, by this time photolithography was past the experimental stage.

PHOTOLITHOGRAPHY

There were two methods of making photolithographs. One involved coating the stone with a solution of bitumen and oil of lavender (later replaced by ether), attempted by Niepce early in the century but not worked successfully until 1852, when four Frenchmen named Barreswill, Davanne, Lerebours and Lemercier succeeded in printing by it. They produced a book, *Lithophotographie*, in 1853 to demonstrate their plates, but the method does not appear to have been used in England and was largely abandoned on the continent in favour of the second, or Poitevin's, method.

In 1855 A. L. Poitevin discovered that potassium bichromate mixed with albumen and gelatine could be used as a light-sensitive substance in lithography. The stone was coated with this material, which became insoluble when exposed to light; it required a shorter exposure time than bitumen; and its unexposed portions could be washed from the stone with water.[7] Poitevin patented this process in 1855 and it was used by Lemercier in France, but was not apparently worked in England.

The first English book with photolithographed illustrations is John Pouncy's *Dorsetshire Photographically Illustrated*, published by subscription in 1857. Pouncy was a photographer and dealer in artists' materials and fancy goods at what he called the Dorchester Photographic Institution. His book came out in four parts in oblong format, most of the plates being about 28cm by 20cm, though one splendid view of Maiden Castle is a double plate. He had originally intended to illustrate the book with pasted-in photographs, but decided against them because of their propensity to fade. Although Pouncy did not publicise his process, various accounts and examples of it appeared in *Photographic Notes* between 1858 and 1863, in which year he patented it (No 267). Thomas Sutton published a book about it, *Photography in Printing Ink*, but by that time it had been superseded by more effective methods.

The sensitive material which Pouncy used consisted of bitumen dissolved in benzole and mixed with printers' ink. He called it 'black stuff'. It was spread on one side of a piece of transparent paper and exposed under a negative which was placed against the uncoated side of the paper. The light passing through the negative caused the 'black stuff' to harden and adhere to the paper backing. After exposure the unhardened portions of the 'black stuff' could be washed away with turpentine, leaving a photographic image of the picture on the negative. The resulting print could be used as a lithographic transfer in the usual way. All the plates in the book have been overprinted with a tint stone whose highlights have been scraped away as usual. The tones appear to have been obtained by graining the stone in the chalk style. It is doubtful if much more than the outlines were actually obtained photographically.

Pouncy did not produce any more books and the next examples of photolithography are plates made by the Ordnance Survey. Photography had been used at their Southampton establishment since about 1855 for the reduction in scale of maps;[7] the photographs were traced by hand and then rubbed down on to the waxed surface of a copper plate. Captain A. de C. Scott was evidently experimenting in the late 1850s to find ways of speeding up this procedure; he first used Pouncy's method to try and produce lithographic prints from the negatives, but did not succeed in obtaining results that were better than fair. In 1857, however, Edward Isaac Asser invented a better transfer method, using bichromate of potash carried by starch, the paper being covered with a thin film of starch or flour paste and immersed in a weak solution of bichromate before being exposed under a negative in the usual way. After exposure it was washed in cold water to remove the unaltered starch, then dried and pressed with a hot iron to harden the exposed portions. The ink, when it was applied, adhered only to the image and could be transferred to a lithographic surface.

The Director of the Ordnance Survey at this time was Colonel Henry James (1803–77) of the Royal Engineers, who had been commissioned in 1826. He had worked in Ireland and Scotland, had been elected a Fellow of the Royal Society in 1848, and was an associate juror for military engineering at the Great Exhibition. He had become Director of the Ordnance Survey in 1854, and his later career included a knighthood in 1860, and promotion to Lieutenant-General before he retired from the OS in 1875. He was enthusiastic about the method Scott had been using, which he called photozincography, as zinc was used as the lithographic printing surface. Scott had, in fact, adopted Asser's method, which was used to print a facsimile of a small deed of Edward I's time that was included in James's Report to Parliament in 1859.[8] Photozincography was used to print a number of facsimiles of manuscripts from 1861 onwards, the most important being *Domesday Book*, 1861-3, *National Manuscripts of England*, 1865-7 and *National Manuscripts of Scotland*, 1867-71.

James published a ten-page pamphlet about photozincography in 1860, but a fuller account was written by Scott and published as *On Photozincography and Other Photographic Processes Employed at the Ordnance Survey Office, Southampton* in 1862. It gives a sufficiently detailed account of the manipulations needed to make photozincographs for others to try their hands at it; it is illustrated with examples of facsimiles and reproductions of engravings which demonstrated that originals could be reduced satisfactorily and that the process was only of use for line work. The term photozincography was not used by most printers, who preferred photolithography to describe the process.

There is little doubt that Asser's discovery made photolithography possible during the 1860s. It is mentioned by S. T. Davenport in a paper published by the Society of Arts in January 1865, and he took his account from the publication of Osborne's method in the *Photographic Journal*.[9] J. W. Osborne discovered his method in Australia at about the same time that James was successful in England. He was head of the Government Survey Office in Melbourne and also used Asser's transfer method with modifications.[10] He first coated the paper with albumen and polished it by passing it through a rolling press or a lithographic press, then coated it with bichromated gelatine, exposed and inked it. The unaltered gelatine was removed by floating the paper on boiling water, which loosened it and allowed it to be sponged away, leaving the outline of the image on the paper. It was then transferred to the lithographic stone. In James's process no albumen was used and the recommended water temperature was only 90°F. Osborne had intended to patent his method, but, when his representative in England called on James, he was told that there was no material difference between the two processes, and James's had already been published.

Another printer working on photolithography at this time was William Griggs (1832–1911), who was to become the greatest chromolithographic printer of the last quarter of the century. He was the son of one of the Duke of Bedford's lodgekeepers and was born at Woburn. He started his working life as an apprentice carpenter, in which capacity he was present at the Indian Court of the Great Exhibition. He became technical assistant to the Director of the Indian Museum in 1855, and was encouraged by his superiors in the study of photography and lithography. He benefited from the publication of James's method and, experimenting to improve it, as no doubt other printers were doing, discovered that if cold water was used in developing the transfer instead of hot the gelatine remained in the white areas of the picture, giving firmer adhesion to the stone and support to the fine lines that were being transferred. Griggs gave a talk to the Photographic Society of London in 1868 explaining his improvements, and in this year set up his own photolithographic works in his house at Peckham. His most important innovation was colour printing by photolithography, in which he achieved extremely high standards. He first printed a very faint impression from a photolitho transfer that comprised most of the outlines of the picture and formed a key for printing on the colours. His colour transfers were obtained by painting out on each negative the unwanted portions, so that the transfer would consist of only the portion of the picture to be printed in one particular shade. These transfers were then used to produce one stone for each colour, and they were printed in order on to the paper. James had used this method in *Domesday Book*, but had not published his technique. Griggs published a pamphlet about his process in 1882 under the title *Illustrated Pamphlet of Photo-chromolithography*, and in that year installed electric light in his studio. He left the India Office, as it had become, in 1885 to run his own business full time, specialising in the making of chromolithographs and collotypes. He was responsible for a considerable number of plates, from those of Forbes Watson's *Textile Manufactures and Costumes of the People of India*, 1866, to the *Journal of Indian Art and Industry*, started in 1884 and still being published after his death. Watson's *Textile Manufactures* contains pasted-in photographs as well as photolithographs, and is thus a tacit admission of the failure of the latter to reproduce tones satisfactorily. The photographs are mostly hand-coloured and show little sign of fading; evidently Griggs was an above average photographer. The same methods of illustration are found in James Fergusson's *Tree and Serpent Worship*, 1868. The high standards of Griggs' chromolithography can be seen in such publications as *Some Minor Arts*, issued by Seeley in 1894, and from a technical point of view, *Illuminated Manuscripts in the British Museum*, 1903. The latter was a folder containing six plates of manuscript miniatures and borders and a series of impressions showing the separations used in printing one of the plates. The first of these separations shows the faint key, and the second the tint stone, printed without the highlights removed. In this series the opaque colours can be seen quite clearly to have been printed first, and the translucent colours printed over them. Two gold printings were used, the medium being pale yellow mixed with gold size: gold leaf was applied directly to the third stone by hand, and gold powder to the nineteenth stone, two quite different impressions of gold resulting from these treatments. The appearance of thick medieval gold leaf was obtained by using embossing for the two last operations. The finished print went through the press twenty-four times.

One early photolithographic firm was Day & Son, examples of whose plates can be seen in the periodical *Nature and Art*,

1866–7, volume 1 at 10s 6d and volume 2 at 8s 6d. The photo-lithographs are all in line, and monochrome, though some of them are printed with a tint stone. Another of Day's publications was *Recollections of the East by a Subaltern*, 1867, an oblong quarto consisting simply of captions and plates, all of them being in line. S. H. L. Hailstone's *Designs for Lacemaking*, 1870, was published by E. J. Francis, whose address was 'Office of the Photochromo-lith'; some of the plates are coloured but only one colour appears on each plate.

Early photolithographs differ so little from ordinary lithographs that it is often difficult to identify them unless they are signed on the plate or mentioned somewhere in the book. Interesting examples appear in Hatton Turnor's *Astra Castra: Experiments and Adventures in the Atmosphere*, 1865, which has photozincographed plates, and T. P. Salt's *A Treatise on Deformities and Debilities of the Lower Extremities* . . ., 1866, which has photolithographs printed by a Birmingham lithographer, T. Underwood. The tones in these plates have been put in by hand; lack of an effective system of tone hampered lithography for some decades. An idea of its progress can be obtained from a series of addresses given to the Society of Arts in the 'Cantor Lectures' series by Thomas Bolas. The first of these was given in the summer of 1878 under the title 'The application of Photography to the Production of Printing Surfaces and Pictures in Pigment', and describes the normal method of transfer photolithography. In spite of the availability of power presses for lithographic printing since Sigl's press of 1852, it was still considered a relatively slow process. In the autumn of 1884 Bolas gave another series of Cantor Lectures on 'Recent Improvements in Photo-mechanical Printing Methods', and, during one of them, he said: 'At the time of my last lecture it was the exception to find a London printer who made use of photo-transfers for litho work . . . or photoetched zinc blocks . . . but now it would be difficult to find a large London printing house where these are not in regular use.'

The number of photolithographers listed in Kelly's *Post Office Directory of Stationers, Printers* . . . increased from five in 1872, when they are first listed, to thirty-five in 1889, after which there is a decline to twenty-nine in 1900.

The lack of an effective halftone method held back photolithography until the end of the century, though a number of efforts were made to overcome this drawback. The first notable progress was made in 1865 by E. & J. Bullock of Leamington (Patent No 2954), who impressed the transfer sheet with the grain from an aquatint plate, and copied the photograph on to it so that the continuous tints were broken up and could be printed as different sized random dots. One of their plates was published in *The Photographic News* for 20 April 1866, captioned 'Lithophotograph from Nature'. Although they claimed to be able to obtain 2,600 prints from one stone at the rate of 500 to 600 a day,[11] their method was little used for book illustration.[12] Bolas, in his lecture of 1884, mentioned the Bullocks' process and showed an example, which he said was as good as anything that had been done since. He asked: 'Why then . . . did not the process become a great thing commercially and make its mark? The answer is simply this—the invention came before its time, neither good litho machining nor zinc-etching being practised at the time . . .' —but his explanation is unconvincing, since litho machining does not appear to have been any worse in the 1860s than at any other time during the century. Although a number of ways of printing photolithos in tone were devised, none of them became commercially acceptable before the invention of the halftone screen in the 1880s, when it became possible to use a screened negative to make a transfer for photolithography, and some printers did so. Since photolithos tended to be printed on the same sort of paper as relief halftones, it is generally rather difficult to spot them unless they are signed. The firm of A. Brothers & Co were certainly using them in the 1890s[13] (Plate 25).

GRAPHOTYPE

Hindsight makes it obvious that photography was to carry all before it in the field of book illustration, but it was not so apparent in the 1860s. At least one quite significant autographic

Plate 25 Screened halftone photolithograph by transfer with some handwork on the stone. A. Brothers, *Photography* (1899)

method was being publicised and used commercially during this decade, and that was graphotype; and, though it was more successful than the others, it was not the only method put forward in England. It was invented by an American artist and wood engraver, De Witt Clinton Hitchcock, of New York, and in England was taken up by Henry Fitz-Cook, who formed a limited company called The Graphotyping Company to promote it. Edward Roper was one of the promoters and the process was patented in the name of B. Day in 1865 (No 664).

The first steps in the invention were taken in the summer of 1860, when Hitchcock was making a drawing on a wood block for engraving. He had to erase part of his drawing, and, to re-whiten the surface of the block, used the 'enamelled' surface of a visiting card, presumably a polished coating of china clay. The surface was removed with a brush and water, and then Hitchcock noticed that the printed letters on the card were standing up in relief. This led him to experiment with a piece of chalk about 1in thick on which he drew with ink made from silicate of potash coloured with indigo. He made a drawing 4in by 6in and changed it into a relief block by rubbing the surface of the chalk with a toothbrush, causing it to disintegrate wherever the ink was not present. He then covered the entire surface of the block with silicate and took a proof from it. He optimistically named the process graphotype, meaning a print made from chalk, but unfortunately the chalk would not stand up to the pressure of the press, even when specially compacted blocks were made with a hydraulic press, and it had to be stereotyped or electro-typed. The compressed chalk block was first burnished and sized. The artist traced his design in reverse on to the block and then filled in the lines with special ink made of glue and lampblack, and then the untouched chalk was removed with brushes of fitch-hair and the whole surface treated with silicate.

The main advantage of the process, stressed by the promoters, was its autographic nature; and an advertisement in *Britannia* for January 1869 claimed that the cost of a graphotype was half that of a wood engraving. The best known book in which graphotype was used was Isaac Watts' *Divine and Moral Songs for Children*, with illustrations by Holman Hunt, published by Nisbet & Co in 1866. The artist was very satisfied with the results, particularly since no wood engraver had been necessary. Examples appeared in *Nature and Art* in December 1866 and *Once a Week* in February 1867. It was used in other books from time to time—*Toby Almanack* for 1868, edited by Percy Cruickshank; H. K. Browne's *Racing and Chasing, the Road, the River and the Hunt*; and Florence Claxton's *The Adventures of a Woman in Search of Her Rights*, both undated. It seems that unsuccessful attempts were made to apply photography to graphotype, for a pamphlet published in 1874 and entitled *Specimens of Photo-graphotype Engraving* claimed that it could be used for copying plates already printed, in a variety of styles. Although examples of this facsimile printing are shown in the pamphlet, no details are given. Apparently The Graphotyping Company eventually failed, since a report in the *Process Photogram* for 1897 says that it was taken over by Dalziel Brothers. Later writers claimed that it was a failure: Bolas wrote in 1884, 'Some years ago the "graphotype" process made a little stir, but it did not compete with wood engraving to any extent . . .', and Carl Hentschel in his paper to the Society of Arts in 1900 mentions graphotype having been used 'some thirty-four years ago' but 'although to a certain degree ingenious and original, it was not found sufficiently practical'.

KEROGRAPHY

Another minor process dating from this period was based on a soft surface that could be electrotyped. It was invented by W. J. Linton and called Kerography or Electrograph; and in view of the first of these names it is likely that the drawing was made through wax and then electrotyped to make the block. Linton published a pamphlet in 1861 called *Specimens of a New Process for Surface Printing*, and the word kerography appears on the outside of the cover. He claimed that the cost was about 2s per square inch. The only book in which the process seems to have been used was a translation by A. Wehnert called *Anderson's Tales for Children*, published by Bell & Daldy in 1869, with illustrations in relief blocks showing perhaps a freer line than was customary with wood engravings.

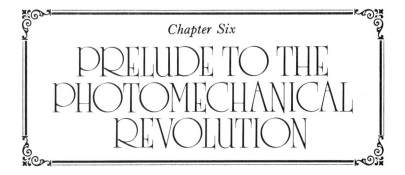

Chapter Six

PRELUDE TO THE PHOTOMECHANICAL REVOLUTION

DURING THE 1870s the foundations were laid for two of the most effective illustrative methods yet devised. The perfecting of the carbon print was to enable photogravure to be developed in the next decade, while the effective manipulation of collotype introduced the most perfect tonal printing system yet seen.

THE CARBON PRINT

The development of the carbon print was documented from a surprisingly early stage, probably because it was envisaged, and doubtless largely used, as a photographic printing method for amateurs who needed books of instruction to which it was customary to preface a short history. The first of these handbooks is G. Wharton Simpson's *On the Production of Photographs in Pigments: Containing Historical Notes on Carbon Printing and Practical Details of Swan's Patent Carbon Process*, 1867. The Swan referred to is Sir Joseph Wilson Swan, who succeeded in making carbon printing a practicable process, perfecting his

99

method after studying the work of Mungo Ponton and Edmond Becquerel.[1] The process was based on Alphonse Poitevin's use in 1855 of powdered carbon mixed with bichromated gelatine;[2] this mixture was spread on paper, exposed under a negative and washed, the blackness of the lines in the resulting picture being proportional to the density of the negative. These pictures would not show any halftones effectively, as all the partially exposed gelatine was removed when the plate was washed. Since exposure was from the top, the light caused the upper portions of the gelatine to harden, but it remained soft underneath and consequently would not adhere to the paper.[3] Pouncy seems to have been the first person to realise that better results could be obtained by exposure through the paper,[4] but the materials he used did not enable him to obtain halftones.

Joseph Wilson Swan (1828–1914) was born at Sunderland and apprenticed to a chemist, but before the end of his apprenticeship he joined the firm of John Mawson, who encouraged him in his study of photography. He was particularly interested in the hardening action of light on bichromated gelatine and started experimenting with carbon prints towards the end of 1858. He soon realised that the gelatine must be exposed on the side that was not going to be washed. He started by coating a glass plate with a mixture of lampblack, gum arabic and bichromate of potash that was exposed through the glass plate,[5] but, although this idea was sound, he could not make it work in practice.[6] Adolphe Fargier, however, made a film that could be removed from its base, which he patented in 1861, and Swan, taking advantage of this invention, used gelatine in the form of a thin film coloured with carbon or other pigment and sensitised with bichromate of potash. The gelatine tissue was generally given a temporary paper backing for ease of handling, and exposed under a negative. After exposure, but before being developed, it was stuck exposed side downwards on to another piece of paper with rubber solution. It was then washed in warm water, which removed the backing paper and then the unexposed portions of the gelatine, and left the hardened pigmented gelatine adhering to its mount in a depth directly proportional to the amount of light that had fallen on to it through the negative. The resulting print thus had a surface of variable height above the paper, the deep areas of carbon appearing dark and the shallow areas light, resulting in perfect halftones.

Swan patented this process in 1864 (No 503) and started working it commercially in 1866.[7] Although he produced a good many prints, he does not seem to have made book illustrations, with the possible exception of the frontispiece to Simpson's *On the Production of Photographs* . . . In 1866 he sold his English patent rights to the Autotype Printing & Publishing Company, formed by W. Benyon Winsor.[8] Swan pursued other aspects of photomechanical printing, in 1865 patenting photomezzotint, an attempt to obtain an electromatrix for casting images with a gelatinous pigment. He was responsible for certain improvements in photography, but is best known for the invention of the incandescent light bulb. He was knighted in 1904 and received numerous other distinctions.

AUTOTYPES

The Autotype Company made certain improvements in Swan's process: one was J. R. Johnson's discovery that it was not necessary to stick the tissue down on its support with adhesive, since it could simply be held in position by suction if all the air and water were removed from between the two[9] (Plate 26). The company evidently aimed at photographic printing for and by amateurs, for they sold licences to practise the process or would process prints themselves. A series of handbooks was published to assist practitioners, one being *The Autotype Process*, first published in 1867 and running into a number of editions up to about 1878. A new version by J. R. Sawyer called *The 'A.B.C.' Guide to the Making of Autotype Prints* appeared in 1887, and it had reached its fifth edition by 1899. The company (today part of the Norcross Group) advertised carbon prints well into the twentieth century.[10] A good deal of its output came to be devoted to the print market, and it had the Autotype Fine Art Gallery at

Autotype Co., London and Ealing Dene.

1. Mounting (use of the Squeegee).

2. Developing the Prints.

3. Fixing in Alum Solution.

A. Cold Water Tray, No. 1.

B. Blotting Boards.

C. Mounting Dish and Stool.

D. Developing Tank.

E. Cold Water Tray, No. 2.

F. Alum Bath.

G. Cold Water Tray, No. 3.

H. "Hero" Stove.

Sawyer's Collotype Process.

J. Johnson's Actinometers.

R. Burton's Actinometers.

S. Sawyer's Actinometers.

T. Pressure Frames.

P. Autotype Pressure Boxes.

V. Packets of Cut Tissues.

W. Waxing Compound.

X. Collodion

Plate 26 Collotype print showing autotype printing.
J. Sawyer, *The 'A.B.C.' Guide to Autotype* (1899). 11 × 17·5cm

74 New Oxford Street, where a print about 43cm by 35cm could be bought for 12s.

Autotypes began to be used in English books in the late 1860s, one of the earliest, signed 'autotype', appearing in Josiah Gilbert's *Cadore, or Titian's Country*, published by Longmans in 1869. Other early examples appeared in B. B. Woodward's *Specimens of the Drawings of Ten Masters*, 1870, for which they were made by Edwards & Kidd, licencees of the company. Another firm of licencees was Cundall & Fleming, which made the autotypes for George Duplessis's *Wonders of Engraving*, 1871. A second issue of this work omitted the autotypes, replacing some of them with steel engravings, and there is some evidence that they were thought unsatisfactory.[11]

In 1871 the Autotype Company published an edition of Turner's *Liber Studiorum*, a collection of prints that attracted a number of publishers in the second half of the century and was reproduced by various processes. William Day had printed a selection of the plates lithographically about 1860 in *Liber Studiorum . . . a Selection of Fifteen of the Best Plates*, but it was not a very successful facsimile, failing to match the bistre shade of the originals, which had been published by Turner as a series of etched and mezzotinted plates from 1807 to 1819. Another facsimile was published in 1861 'under the authority of the Department of Science and Art', with thirty gold-toned albumen prints.[12]

The autotype version of 1871 had the advantage of a wider range of colours than was available for the albumen prints, and its prints make a good match with the originals. It was also able to present a matt surface quite like the original, and it was complete, which the other versions were not. It is disappointing, however, because of certain errors of production and others inherent in the process. Autotype prints shrank slightly on drying and so the prints are slightly smaller than the originals, though this fact is not mentioned anywhere in the volumes. Even worse it was bound up in conventional book shape, 36cm by 28cm, whereas the original is oblong, and consequently all the plates had to be

Plate 27 Autotype reproduction of Turner's *Liber Studiorum* (1871).
17·5 × 25cm

inserted sideways. Being stuck on to pages of thick stiff paper
divorced the prints further from their originals (Plate 27). The
company produced a greatly improved edition in 1882–3, when
someone went to considerable trouble to produce a closer facsimile. Although the plates are described as autotypes, they are
actually collotypes printed on a rough-surfaced paper, much
closer to the handmade paper of the original, and with toned
backgrounds extended round the pictures to give the impression
of a plate mark. This edition was issued in three volumes like the
earlier one, at 4 guineas a volume, though it probably was not a
great success at this price, for the remaining stock of plates were
issued as a 'limited edition' of 150 copies in 1899.

By this time the Victorians must have been accustomed to

pasted-in illustrations, however cumbersome they appear to us. One book that goes some way towards overcoming the problem is *The Landseer Gallery*, published by George Bell in 1875, with twenty autotypes of Landseer's terrible anthropomorphic paintings. They are not direct reproductions of the originals but taken from engravings and mounted complete with plate mark, the latter tending to disguise to some extent the pasting-on process. Tone in autotypes is very good, better than in the originals in the case of steel engravings, as the fine lines tend to be run together by the camera and are less noticeable. This effect is particularly advantageous in the reproduction of an oil painting.

Autotypes used for book illustration are generally larger than silver prints, and were presumably easier, or cheaper, to print in these sizes. The variety of colour available was also greater, the Turner being printed in bistre and the Landseer in sepia, and, above all, they were permanent. Unfortunately for autotypes all these advantages were enjoyed by woodburytypes, which were considerably cheaper, though the former continued to be used in book illustration as late as the 1890s. *Alfred Stevens and His Work* by Hugh Stannus used autotypes to reproduce chalk drawings, and they are as good as the originals. Stannus remarked in his book that the term 'autotype' was 'applied to carbon printing by Mr Tom Taylor (an art critic of some authority in his day)'.

WOODBURYTYPES

Although carbon prints were not extensively used for book illustration, their invention resulted in two processes which were very frequently used—woodburytypes and photogravure. The former began to appear in the 1860s, but were most numerous during the following decade. In appearance they are very like autotypes, having the same high tonal qualities, due to their photo-relief manufacture, and the same disadvantage of having to be pasted in. They were invented by Walter Bentley Woodbury, who was born in Manchester in 1834, and, after being apprenticed to learn engineering, left England in 1852 for the

Australian goldfields, where he was not very successful. He finished up with a job at the Melbourne waterworks, where he practised photography as a hobby, then went to the Dutch East Indies as a photographer, finally returning to England in 1863. He settled in Birmingham and experimented with carbon printing, demonstrating his application of it to the Photographic Society in 1865. He patented what became known as woodburytypes in a series of patents in 1866 and 1867.[13] The process required much expensive equipment, and he was trying to develop a simpler version called stannotype when he died at Margate from an overdose of laudanum in September 1885.

Woodbury had practised the wet collodion process in the East Indies and was a practised photographer when Swan patented his carbon printing process. Like others, Woodbury was searching for a remedy to the fading of photographic prints. His first attempts involved making carbon prints in much the same way as Swan, but, instead of stopping there and using the pigmented photo-relief gelatine to make his picture, he attempted to use it in a moulding process, first using an electrotype as a mould[14]—an unsatisfactory method, as Swan also found. Woodbury first mentioned the use of the carbon relief to indent a lead mould in patent No 1918 of July 1866, and established a practicable method of doing this by 1867.

In making a woodburytype the pigmented light-sensitive gelatine was spread thickly on a glass plate, since a high relief was required in the carbon print to make a satisfactory mould, and the print was given a lengthy exposure through a negative made with strong contrast, preferably in full sunshine. After exposure the gelatine leaf was separated from the glass when fully developed, in the usual manner with carbon prints, and was then left to contract for a while.

The lead moulds were manufactured in a hydraulic press at a pressure of 4 tons per square inch, the largest size that could reasonably be made being a whole plate, requiring a pressure of 200 tons.[15] The carbon print was placed on a piece of smooth steel about 1in thick in the bed of the press, and the lead for

Plate 28   Woodburytype press made by Smith & Coventry of Manchester. Crown Copyright. Science Museum, London

the mould placed above it. Actuating the press drove the lead down on to the gelatine and formed the mould, a method of making a mould similar to that used in Auer's method of nature printing. About six moulds could be obtained from each carbon print.[16]

The print was reproduced in a mixture of gelatine, water and colouring matter. Indian ink was recommended for amateurs (there cannot have been many of them) but commercial operators used various pigments to produce a range of colours, mainly dark blues and dark browns, but occasionally terra cotta. The mixture consisted of one part of gelatine to five parts of water in summer, with slightly more water in winter.

The mould was first wiped out with an oily cloth and the mixture poured into it to form a pool about half the diameter of the picture; the paper was laid on top, and pressure applied. A special press was required so that the print could be left for a short time to allow the gelatine to set (Plate 28). When removed, the print was immersed for five minutes in a 3 per cent solution of alum to make it insoluble.[17] About 1,000 impressions could be taken from one lead mould. In commercial practice the small presses for making prints were mounted on turntables in sets of six, enabling the operator to remove a dried print and pour in gelatine for a fresh one while the other five dried. Apart from the capital cost of the presses, this was a very economical way of printing pictures. Woodburytypes were much cheaper than auto-types and could be made more quickly.[18]

Woodbury sold his patent rights to companies in France and America, and tried to do so in this country, apparently not wishing to exploit the invention himself; but Disdéri & Company, his English purchasers, failed to pay the fees, and so he set up the Woodbury Permanent Printing Company, which printed illustrations for a number of publications. As its prices were lower than other photographic processes, the method was very successful (Plate 29). *The Picture Gallery Annual*, published principally for the illustrations, around which the text was written, cost 18s in 1873 and contained forty-eight woodburytypes.[19] Few of the pictures were taken directly from the originals, apart from pictures of statues, but were photographed from wood engravings, steel engravings or lithographs. Numerous books were illustrated in the 1870s with woodburytypes, not only art books, but books containing portraits, and others on topography and travel. An

CHARLES J. BRENAN, PHOTO.   *Woodburytype.*

CRAB INN, SHANKLIN, ISLE OF WIGHT.

Printed by THE WOODBURY COMPANY (EYRE AND SPOTTISWOODE), 6, Great New Street, London, E.C.

Plate 29 Woodburytype from A. Brothers, *Photography* (1899).
10 × 14·5cm

example of a travel book that exploits the potentialities of the process was R. B. Tristram's *Pathways of Palestine*, 1881, which used topographical photographs taken direct from their subjects; the plates measure about 18cm by 13cm, and were printed in a purplish-brown colour to look like silver prints; and with forty prints this book sold for 31s 6d. One of the books most lavishly illustrated with woodburytypes was *Men of Mark, a Gallery of Contemporary Portraits*, 1876–83, which had 252.

The process was used by a number of firms in the 1880s: Waterlow's, who exhibited it at the International Exhibition in

1885 and were still advertising it in 1894;[20] the London Stereo-scopic & Photographic Company; and Lock & Whitfield, who were responsible for the twenty-nine prints in *The Trees and Shrubs of Fife and Kinross* by J. Jeffrey and C. Howie, privately printed and published at Leith in 1879. After Woodbury's death the Woodbury Company came into the hands of Eyre & Spottis-woode, who were advertising it in 1898, particularly for wood-burygravures, which were primarily intended for use in book illustration. These were not developed until the 1890s, how-ever, too late to be used very much. They had a matt surface and were transferred directly on to the pages of the book, so as to be less obvious in appearance; but the verso of the page always showed that something had been fixed rather than printed on the other side (Plate 30).

Various continental printers used woodburytypes, and the process was also used in America.[21] The last surviving equip-ment was owned by Braun of Dornach, and acquired by J. M. Eder for the Graphische Lehr-und Versuchsanstaldt in Vienna, where it was used until 1928 for teaching purposes and then sold as scrap.

It is fairly simple to distinguish a woodburytype from a pasted-in photograph, for the latter is more likely to be found in a book published before 1868 and the former in one published after about 1870. The surface of a woodburytype is never absolutely smooth; sometimes the variation in thickness can be seen quite easily, but, even when it cannot, there is an absence of smoothness about the surface which can be seen when the light is reflected off it. Furthermore, woodburytypes never faded round the edges as most photographs of this period did.

COLLOTYPE

What were, in the event, to be more significant advances were marked in England by two patents taken out in 1869—No 3049 of 19 October in the name of F. R. Window, and No 3543 of 8 December in that of Ernest Edwards, both for collotype pro-cesses. The history of collotype on the continent is well docu-

Woodbury-Gravure.   L. M. RUTHERFURD, *Photo.*

THE MOON—FIRST QUARTER.

Printed by THE WOODBURY COMPANY (EYRE AND SPOTTISWOODE), 6, Great New Street, London, E.C.

Plate 30   Woodburygravure from A. Brothers, *Photography*
(1899). 14·5 × 10cm

mented.[22] Its basic principle, discovered by A. L. Poitevin and patented in December 1855 (No 2815), is that metal or glass coated with bichromated gelatine exposed under a negative and then moistened with water will accept greasy ink in proportion to the amount of light falling on it; and that, as the gelatine dries, it reticulates, producing a fine grain on the surface of the printing plate, whose tone is obtained by the blackness of the resulting irregular dots. F. Joubert produced some prints by this method, calling them phototypes, and one was presented with the June 1860 issue of the *Photographic Journal*; but they were never used for book illustration.

C. M. Tessié du Motay & C. R. Maréchal of Metz took out an English patent (No 712 of 14 March) in 1865 for a method using a copper-plate base, but it does not appear to have been used to illustrate English books.

Three people arrived, apparently independently, at a practicable process. The earliest was Joseph Albert of Bavaria, whose process, which he called albertype, was the basis of the later commercial collotype; the second was Jakob Husnik of Prague, who introduced a process very similar to Albert's and was bought out by the latter to remove competition;[23] the third was Ernest Edwards, who called his method heliotype.

Albertypes were little used for book illustration in England, though examples appear in Hermann Vogel's *The Chemistry of Light and Photography*, published by H. S. King in 1876 ('new and revised edition' of the first edition of 1872). Vogel thought both albertypes and woodburytypes inferior to silver prints, though the former, when varnished, look at a casual glance very like silver prints, if they are pasted in, as they were in the *Chemistry of Light*. A specimen presented with the *Photographic News* of 24 June 1870, and entitled 'Albertype, a new photomechanical printing process', shows the interior of Albert's printing shop.

F. R. Window's patent No 3049 of 1869 was originally taken out by Ohm & Grossman of Berlin. Window was the agent for, or possibly involved in, the Autotype Company, the first English firm to market collotype. The work was done by a subsidiary[24] called Spencer, Sawyer, Bird & Company, of which J. R. Sawyer seems to have been the most enterprising member. Some of their prints are described as 'Sawyer's collotype', and his 'Photography in the Printing Press', a paper read to the London Photographic Society and published in the *Photographic Journal* in January 1872, and elsewhere, was the first account by an English practitioner.

The main difficulty in early collotype was making the gelatine film adhere sufficiently well to its base for a reasonable number of impressions to be taken. The surface of the gelatine needed to be as hard as possible to stand up to the wear and tear of printing. A great number of minor variations on the process were used, but basically it remained much the same during the last quarter of the century.

A good account of how collotype printers worked was published by W. T. Wilkinson in 1888.[25] A ground-glass surface was produced by sprinkling emery powder and water on two glass plates and rubbing them together, 'Good British plate at least a quarter of an inch thick' being recommended. When ready, the plates were washed and dried before being covered with a mixture of stale beer, water, and silicate of soda and dried at 150°F in an oven. While still warm the plate to be used was covered with the sensitive solution of bichromated gelatine, and then returned to the oven for two or three hours to dry at 120°F. It could be used for up to three weeks afterwards if kept dark and away from damp. The plates were prepared for printing by exposure under a reversed negative. When the front had been exposed, the back of the printing frame was removed and the light allowed to fall on the back of the ground-glass plate, which hardened the gelatine below the surface and helped to weld gelatine and glass together. The plate was finally washed in cold water to remove the bichromate, and allowed to dry thoroughly before use.

The first collotype printers used lithographic presses. The plate was sponged with cold water, dried off with blotting paper, and inked with a lithographer's leather roller. Sawyer stated that they sometimes used two or more inks of varying degrees of stiffness, and commented that 'the operation of printing is one requiring delicacy, taste, and skill in the rolling'. Wilkinson recommended soaking the plates with a solution of glycerine in water before printing, and stated that they could be printed on an Albion or Columbian press, though he recommended a lithographic press. By the time he was writing, power presses were available for collotype. They were advertised by several firms, mainly German—Hugo Koch, and Schmiers, Werner & Stein, both of Leipzig, for example. The earliest examples had been made by Faber & Company of Offenbach, but were apparently too complicated and delicate in construction to be successful.[26] Two plates in Wilkinson's book are captioned 'Printed by steam on Alauzet & Co.'s collotype machine', Alauzet being a Paris firm that also made hand machines. In both hand and power presses the impression was by roller, and the examples in Wilkinson's book are perfectly satisfactory. Roller presses quadrupled the life of the plate, compared to lithographic scraper presses, and were capable of inking it up to three times, although multiple inking shortened its life. Between 800 and 1,500 impressions a day could be taken.[27]

Waterlow & Sons established a collotype printing department, which was managed by George S. Waterlow, who started it about 1883, Paul Waterlow and J. D. Geddes. In 1884 they imported two of the largest collotype machines, one by Schmiers, Werner & Stein of Leipzig and the other by Alauzet & Company, and these are said to have been the first steam machines in use in England.

In their publications the Autotype Company often failed to distinguish between autotypes and collotypes, so that many early collotypes are signed 'Autotype' in the margin or near the edge of the plate. Some of the earliest books to use it failed to exploit the high tonal qualities collotype offered, among them R. T. Pritchett's *Brush Notes in Holland*, 1871, and Digby Wyatt's *Architect's Note Book in Spain*, 1872, 'with one hundred of the author's sketches reproduced by the autotype mechanical process'. An example using halftones is E. M. Goulburn's *Norwich*

Cathedral, 1876. Sometimes the confusion in terminology found its way on to the title page, as in John Lindley & W. Hutton's *Illustrations of Fossil Plants . . . being an Autotype Reproduction of Selected Drawings*, 1877, actually illustrated with collotypes.

Although the Autotype Company was the earliest practitioner of collotype in this country, one of the independent discoverers was close behind it. Ernest Edwards patented heliotype on 8 December 1869, just after Window had secured his patent. The two methods were similar, but Edwards' lecture to the Society of Arts in 1871 showed how they differed. He toughened the gelatine film by the addition of chrome alum and removed it from the glass plate to expose it under the negative in order to obtain better contact between the two. The gelatine film was fixed on a metal plate by suction during printing, and removed after the impression had been taken. He preferred to print on a platen press, such as an Albion, and used two inks of different texture— a stiff ink for the deep colour areas and a thinner one for the halftones. He claimed that he could obtain over 1,500 impressions from one printing plate. It took about an hour to make a plate and one man could print from 200 to 300 impressions in a day. Edwards claimed that 'book illustrations octavo size could be supplied ready for the binder at 1½d each; smaller sizes would cost more, comparatively speaking, because the labour would be almost as great; but larger sizes less, in proportion'.

Edwards was in partnership with R. L. Kidd,[28] with whom he had produced carbon prints under licence from the Autotype Company. Edwards & Kidd were eventually taken over by the Heliotype Company, which issued a prospectus in 1870 announcing that it had acquired their patents, stock and business. Heliotypes appear in books from 1871, in which year they were used to illustrate Darwin's *Expression of the Emotions in Man and Animals*[29] and *Sun Pictures, a Series of Twenty Heliotype illustrations*, published by Sampson Low. A number were also used in J. Charles Cox's *Notes on the Churches of Derbyshire*, 1875–9; in volume 1 they are signed B. J. Edwards & Co, but later prints in volumes 3 and 4 are signed H. M. Wright & Co.

Collotypes are found in books under a variety of different names. C. T. Newton's *Antiquities of Cyprus*, published by Mansell in 1873 is illustrated with plates that look like collotypes but are signed 'Alethetype'. J. H. Slessor's *The Church of St. Swithin*, 1888, has collotypes signed 'Photophane', which probably refers only to the name of the printers, The Photophane Co. Collotype printers appear in Kelly's *Post Office Directory of Stationers, Printers* . . . for the first time in 1896, when nine firms are listed, though most of them were given earlier under different headings and it is doubtful whether any of them worked collotype alone. In the 1900 edition fourteen firms are listed.

Colour printing by collotype has never been a cheap or easy operation, and, according to R. M. Burch,[30] a reliable source, was more widely practised on the continent than in England. Waterlow's are said to have first used the process in this country, printing some plates for a periodical, *Land and Water*, from August 1891. It was also used by William Griggs, whose plates appear in *Some Minor Arts*, published by Seeley, 1894. Some very attractive work was done by the German printers who printed the plates in Colvin's *Ninety Three Drawings by Dürer*, 1894; a considerable technical achievement is to be found in J. J. Tyler's *Wall Drawings and Monuments of El Kab: the Tomb of Paheri*, 1895, a cumbrous volume which has some coloured collotypes measuring 55cm by 37cm.

Although the 1890s was the decade in which full tone first became practicable in a printing as opposed to a photographic process, the results were not at first as successful as generations of experimentors had anticipated. Woodburytypes and carbon prints both had to be pasted in and, though attractive in themselves, rarely fitted into any concept of book design. Collotypes were better, since they could be inserted as plates.

The progress of collotype possibly had been hampered until the 1890s by patent restrictions and there is some evidence that it was regarded as a secret method: a short report in the *British Lithographer* in 1895, in fact, stated that Richmond Collotype had entered into a partnership with another firm to acquire and turn to account the secret and process of collotype printing. Certainly it was not until the 1890s that many firms were prepared to invest in a process calling for above average skill, for collotype is the finest method of printing pictures and at its best was used in some great books. F. Rathbone's *Old Wedgwood*, 1893–8, with delicately printed reproductions by Griggs (from 1896, previously by Parrot of Paris) can stand comparison with any colour illustrated book of the century.

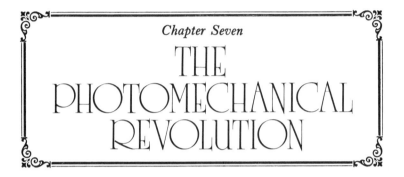

Chapter Seven

THE
PHOTOMECHANICAL
REVOLUTION

INTAGLIO PRINTING plates were the first to be made successfully
by photographic means. The earliest surviving example is a
print of Cardinal d'Amboise made by Nicephore Niepce in 1827,
a heliograph printed on to metal and etched in 1827 by Lemaître,
a Paris engraver. The plate survived and was used by L-D.
Blanquard-Evrard to illustrate the second edition of his *La
Photographie, Ses Origines, Ses Progrès, Ses Transformations,*
1870.[1]

Daguerreotypes, which presented a reversed image on a metal
plate, must have seemed full of potential as intaglio printing
plates, but attempts to etch them and make prints for book
illustration came to very little. Fox Talbot was experimenting in
the early 1850s to find a method of printing his negatives that
would prove more permanent than calotypes had done, but,
although he seems to have had the right ideas, he was unable to
put them into practice commercially. His light-sensitive material
was bichromated gelatine, whose use he patented in 1852.[2] He

reported on his method in the *Athenaeum* and *Photographic Journal* in 1853, and from his accounts it is apparent that he used a steel plate spread with bichromated gelatine, the object to be reproduced (he suggested a leaf) being placed over the treated steel in a photographic frame and exposed. The bichromate would become insoluble where the light fell on it, the unexposed parts could be washed away with cold water and the plate etched with bichloride of platinum. He suggested using this method with a photographic negative and two pieces of black gauze or crêpe to print down a screen on to the plate, but seems only to have done this with a leaf, which, after etching and printing, 'when beheld by the eye at a certain distance appears uniformly shaded, but when examined closely is found to be covered with lines . . .'.[3] He thought that better results would be obtained by using a sheet of glass covered with fine lines or dots and specks, the idea behind the later halftone screen. Talbot called this method 'photoglyptic engraving', and it was used for one plate which he made himself and presented to the *Photographic News* in 1858.[4]

PHOTOGALVANOGRAPHY

One inventor who was working on the production of photo-intaglio plates at this time in England was Paul Pretsch. He proceeded up a blind alley with considerable ingenuity in the painstaking manipulation of an uncommercial but attractive process he called photogalvanography. In his method the tones were obtained from the reticulations on gelatine, as they are in collotype; but instead of applying the principle of lithographic printing to the variations in solubility of exposed bichromated gelatine, he utilised its tendency to swell where unexposed, the degree of swelling being proportionate to the amount of light that fell on it. From the gelatine he made an electrotype and from that another electrotype, the latter, an intaglio plate, having deep areas where the original picture was dark and high areas where it was light, and its surface being divided up into a cellular pattern by the reticulation of the gelatine. It could thus be inked, wiped, and printed from like any other intaglio plate. It was extremely difficult, however, to make these plates, which generally required retouching by hand before they could be used. Pretsch was born in Vienna in 1808, and became a printer, joining the Imperial State Printing Office under Alois Auer in 1842. No doubt it was there that he acquired his skill in electrotyping, having worked on the nature printing process, which depended on it. He was in charge of the Austrian exhibit at the Great Exhibition in 1851, but he left Vienna in 1854 and came to England. He took out a patent for his process (No 2373) in 1854, and it was used for the plates in a publication called *Photographic Art Treasures*, that appeared from 1856 to 1857 in parts, with four plates in each. They were fairly large, measuring 39cm by 58cm. A prospectus for the publication issued by Letts, Son & Co of 8 Royal Exchange, London, lists each part in three states—choice proofs 10s 6d, proofs 7s 6d and prints 5s. Photogalvanography, although it made an early appearance on the photomechanical scene, cannot really be considered a success,[5] though it was quite practicable, as A. & C. Dawson showed in an example they made for A. Brothers' *Photography, Its History, Processes, Apparatus, and Materials*, 1899. By this time, however, swelled gelatine was a commoner material than it had been in Pretsch's day, and doubtless printers were more experienced in handling it (Plate 31).

HELIOGRAVURE

Fox Talbot's basic discovery of photomechanical line etching seems to have been applied with modifications to book illustration by various continental workers, and their plates occasionally found their way into books published in England. G. Scamoni of St Petersburg used bichromated gelatine to make illustrations (called heliographs) in line, something for which it was admirably suited,[6] and two of them, one intaglio and one relief electrotype, were used as illustrations in Hermann Vogel's *Chemistry of Light and Photography* in 1876.

Some English books were illustrated with photo-intaglio prints in line, but they date mainly from the 1880s, though there is so

Plate 31   Pretsch's process (Photogalvanography) printed by A. & C. Dawson for A. Brothers, *Photography* (1899). 7·5 × 10·5cm

little difference between hand-made and photographic prints of this nature that earlier examples may have simply passed unnoticed. J. Leitch & Co worked a line process they called photogravure, and exhibited it at the Caxton Exhibition in 1877,[7] but no details of it seem to have been made available.

In France various experimenters tried to make photomechanical plates in intaglio. One of the earliest was Amand-Durand, who made a number of illustrations that were used in English books under the name of heliogravures, and very similar plates were made by Dujardin.[8] These heliogravures achieved a very high standard of line reproduction; they could be used to make facsimiles of etchings and engravings, as they were in Hamerton's *Drawing and Engraving*, 1892, or for the reproduction of original drawings. Most of Sir George Reid's drawings that appeared as book illustrations were reproduced in this way, his *The River*

Plate 32 Heliogravure of the Broomielaw by Amand-Durand.
G. Reid, *The River Clyde* (1886). 19 × 23cm

Clyde, 1886 (Plate 32), having very delicate heliogravures by
Amand-Durand.

Heliogravures were made by pressing a carbon print that had
been made under a positive transparency on to the printing plate,
removing the paper backing, and leaving an image in soluble
lines that could be washed away with hot water. The hardened
gelatine then formed a resist and the plate could be etched in
the usual way. Herbert Denison in his *Treatise on Photogravure*,
published about 1895, recommended that a ground should be
used even with line plates, but it is difficult to see that this was
necessary.

GOUPIL'S PHOTOGRAVURE

The earliest toned photogravure process which is found other

than rarely in English books is that known by the name of
Goupil. This method was Woodbury's and was based on woodburytype,[9] but Adolphe Goupil's name came to be attached to
it because he had bought the woodburytype patent from Woodbury for 150,000 francs in 1867. In this process a metal plate was
sensitised with a mixture of gum, glucose and bichromate, and
exposed under a positive transparency. The mixture remained
tacky in the dark areas but not in the highlights, with a gradation
of tackiness in the tones. It was then sprinkled with emery
powder or ground glass, the coarse particles of which adhered in
the dark areas and the fine particles in the light areas. The
gradation was obtained by the mixture remaining moist in
inverse proportion to the amount of light falling on it. Once the
gelatine had been grained in this way, a woodburytype lead
mould was made from it and used to make a relief electrotype.
Finally an intaglio electrotype was made and this formed the
actual printing surface. The amount of relief obtained was not
very great and plates made in this manner required a good deal
of working over by hand,[10] which can generally be seen on the
plate. The method worked because the rough grains in the gelatine caused cells to be formed in the mould and these allowed
the electrotype to hold the ink.

The prints were made by Goupil & Cie of Paris (later Valadon,
Boussod & Cie), principally for the print market since the handwork necessary made them expensive for book illustration.[11] The
firm exhibited its prints at the Caxton Exhibition in 1877, one
being in colour.[12]

This method was certainly in use in England by 1879 under
the name of photomezzotint, some obscure verses entitled *The
Epic of Hades* being published in that year with seventeen photo-
mezzotints by George Chapman (Plate 33). A steel plate was
used, and the light-sensitive compound was made from bichromate of ammonia, honey, albumen and water.[13] Details of similar
methods were published during the 1880s by Major Waterhouse, E. W. Foxlee and others,[14] but whether they were ever
used for book illustration is problematical.

Plate 33   Photomezzotint from *The Epic of Hades* (1879).
15 × 10·5cm

PHOTOGRAVURE

The most effective method of toned photogravure was achieved by combining the principles of Talbot's 1858 patent, which contained provisions for etching with ferric chloride solutions of diminishing strength, and the variable resist made available by Swan's patent of 1864. It took some years of experiment by various people before a workable commercial method was obtained, and the man responsible for it was a Czech, Karl Klič.

Karl Klič[15] was born at Arnau in Bohemia in 1841; he showed artistic talent as a boy and was sent to study at the Academy of Arts in Prague. In 1857 he began to study photography and in 1866 founded a satirical newspaper that was quickly suppressed by the Austro-Hungarian government. Klič, however, continued to contribute caricatures and cartoons to other periodicals, and in 1867 went to Vienna, where he worked on various humorous periodicals. He was a wood engraver himself, but he became dissatisfied with the process for the reproduction of his own drawings, and started making relief etchings on zinc, finally setting up his own business. He experimented unsuccessfully with halftone screens, and made halftone blocks using grain screens instead of cross line, but still without much success. A remark made at a meeting of the Vienna Photographic Society in 1876 by G. Märkl seems to have led him to experiment with a carbon print as a variable resist and to think of using intaglio plates; and around 1888 he had succeeded in applying a dust ground to a copper plate and etching it through a carbon print. By 1880 he was receiving medals for his photogravures and sold the secret to the Imperial Printing Office of Vienna in 1881 and to other continental firms in the following years. Thomas Annan of Glasgow bought the process in 1883, and set up Annan & Swan, with Sir Joseph Wilson Swan, in London. Klič visited London in 1888 to supervise his process, while Swan was also actively interested in the application of his carbon tissue to photogravure and frequently offered technical advice.[16]

Klič's process was introduced into America through the agency of Ernest Edwards, who had gone there in 1872 after Edwards & Kidd had been bought up by the Heliotype Company. He founded the Photo-Gravure Company of New York in 1884.

After a certain amount of experimenting Klič succeeded in replacing the dust ground by a cross-line screen with opaque squares and clear lines, and printing it on the carbon tissue before the latter was exposed to the transparency. The principal advantage, apart from simplifying the process, was to enable rotary printing to be used. This meant that printing could be speeded up from 400 or so impressions a day to about 5,000.[17]

Rotary gravure, or rotogravure, was first applied to textile printing. In 1890 Klič was living in Accrington and through a Dr Garland, who also lived there, he was put in touch with the firm of Storey Brothers, textile printers of Lancaster. A provisional agreement was made in that year between Storey's and Klič that his methods should be applied to textile printing; and in 1891 he instructed Samuel Fawcett, who had been experimenting with photo-engraving at Storey's before he met Klič, in the process at Accrington, and went to Lancaster to start installing the machinery. Production by rotogravure printing started in 1893.

Both Klič and the Storeys were interested in art, and, realising that the new method could be applied to printing on paper, they started printing pictures in this way, the reproductions being called 'Rembrandt' prints. In 1895 a subsidiary company, The Rembrandt Intaglio Printing Co, was established to produce them in monochrome. Occasionally they are found as book illustrations, E. Bögh's *Pilgrimage of Truth*, published by Sonnenschein in 1895, being an early example. Experiments were made to print rotogravures in colour, but it is unlikely that any were used in books before the end of the century.

Both Klič and the Storeys kept rotogravure a close secret, and the former was taken into partnership when the venture was established. It is pleasant to record that the relations between them remained good until Klič's death in 1926. The Storeys sent him food during World War I—he had returned to Vienna in

1897—and repaid his capital, which was confiscated as enemy property by the British government.

An account of Klič's process had appeared in *Photographic News* in 1884, and, since he had not patented it, a number of printing firms tried it out. Books started appearing with photogravure plates in 1883, one title being Edmund Gosse's *Critical Essay on the Life and Works of George Tinworth*, published by The Fine Art Society Ltd. The process quickly went into common use and by 1890 the first detailed book about it had appeared —W. T. Wilkinson's *Photogravure*. Herbert Denison's *A Treatise on Photogravure* [1895] gave detailed instructions for both line and tone work, and contains an interesting chapter on the history of photogravure, written by Thomas Bolas. Thomas Huson in *Photoaquatint and Photogravure*, 1897, suggested that the former term should be used for hand-printed plates and the latter for machine. He knew about rotary printing of gravure, but he does not mention the use of the screen, though one of the illustrations in the book is a screened print.

Although the terms used by Huson did not catch on, they are useful to distinguish unscreened from screened photogravure. The general method of proceeding with the former was first to cover a copper plate with an aquatint ground, then dust it with a fine asphaltum powder and heat it to melt the particles on to the plate.[18] Laying the ground was a dirty job and it was difficult to keep the grains standard.[19] The carbon tissue was prepared in the usual way and pressed on to the plate, after which the backing was removed and the soluble gelatine washed away. The plate was then etched with ferric chloride, the etching medium biting through the shallow areas of hardened gelatine more quickly than through the deep areas. As progress was made, solutions of successively less density were used to control the biting more easily. When finished and cleaned, the surface of the plate would be covered with tiny pits whose depth was proportional to the darkness of that part of the picture.

One firm able to experiment with photogravure was the Autotype Company, since it marketed the carbon tissue used by other operators. They called their method 'autogravure', and were using it by 1888 (and possibly earlier) when it was used for the illustrations in H. A. Howell's *The Italian Masters*. The preface of Hugh Stannus's *Alfred Stevens and His Work*, 1891, contains a short account of autogravure, which seems to have varied in little but name from ordinary photogravure. The carbon tissue was called 'special autogravure' tissue and was recommended by most writers on the subject. It was sold in bands 30in wide and 12ft long at 15s in 1900, the smallest quantity supplied being 3ft at 4s 6d.

There was some colour printing by photogravure before the end of the century, not by photomechanical means but by inking the plates carefully by hand with tampons, though it does not seem to have been practised in England. English publishers used French plates: Goupil's were used for Skelton's *Charles I*, 1898; Holmes' *Queen Victoria*, 1897;[20] and for *Great Masters of the Louvre Gallery*, 1899–1900—aesthetically a wonderful achievement, though only twenty-five copies were available for the English market.

Photogravure plates were often retouched by hand; W. T. Wilkinson in *Photo-engraving . . . & Photogravure*, 5th ed [1894], says the highlights could be burnished and the shadows strengthened with a fine roulette, but recommends that the halftones should be left alone. The copper plates were generally steel-faced for book production.

An advertisement for the London Photogravure Syndicate, 5 Victoria Grove, SW, issued after 1891 and now in the John Johnson Collection, gives a list of charges for photogravure work. The minimum charge per plate was 4 guineas, plates up to 13in by 12in were charged at 2s 6d per square inch, and plates larger than that at 3s per square inch.

One moderately successful intaglio process used occasionally in books was Dawson's positive etching, which could apparently be used either as an autographic or as a photomechanical method. In bookwork only the second method seems to have been used. A carbon print on glass was made from the negative and given a thin coating of gold, and it was then electrotyped to make a copper printing plate in intaglio. Although the method was not kept secret, there was evidently more to it than this, since a plate made in this way would not hold the ink; at some stage a mezzotint ground was applied in order to overcome this difficulty, but this part of the manipulation was kept secret—possibly a granulated material was applied to the carbon print at the gold-coating stage.[21] Two books illustrated by Dawson's positive etching were J. Comyns Carr's *Drawings by the Old Masters* [1882], and W. Bemrose's *Joseph Wright*, published by Bemrose of Derby in 1885 with four plates and two etchings. The method was expensive according to Comyns Carr, who said 'it cannot, of course, rank among the more economical modes of book illustration'.

One printer who apparently attempted to make photographic intaglio plates was Duncan C. Dallas; he had worked for Kronheim when they were using Baxter's process[22] and later worked with Pretsch. He took up galvanography after Pretsch's patent lapsed in 1860, having previously attempted to patent a similar process in 1856.[23] He presented an example of his work to the *Photographic News* in 1864, calling it 'dallastype', but it does not seem to have been used in books at this time. Pretsch returned to Vienna in 1865 and Dallas formed a company in 1869, but his blocks are not to be found before the 1880s, by which time he was making relief and planographic blocks. He appears to have changed the names of his processes as time went on, since dallastype came to be applied to relief printing. According to an advertisement in the *Post Office Guide* for 1872, dallastype blocks cost 4d to 6d per square inch for black and white and 8d to 10d per square inch for colour.

LINE BLOCKS

Photomechanical relief blocks had become much more common than intaglio by the 1880s, but the date of their introduction into bookwork in England is obscure, partly because it is difficult to identify them. By the time they came into use wood engravings were also largely printed from electrotypes and no difference can be seen by examining the impression unless the wood block was cracked.

There were two main methods of producing line blocks in use during the last two decades of the century, both of them being developed during the 1860s and 1870s; one was based on Poitevin's discovery that unexposed bichromated gelatine swelled when it came into contact with water, and the other on paneiconography, invented in 1850 by Firmin Gillot (Plate 34). The latter was originally an autographic or transfer method of making a relief block by etching, and became known by the more convenient name of gillotage. The credit for applying photography to gillotage is generally given to Charles Gillot, Firmin's son,[24] but C. Motteroz in his *Essai sur les Gravures Chimiques en Relief*, Paris, 1871, says M. Lefman was the first to apply paneiconography to photo-engraving.[25] Eder says that Charles Gillot abandoned the transfer method in favour of direct photo-printing on zinc in 1872. Line blocks seem first to have been used in France in periodical publications like *L'Art pour Tous*, 1861–91, and *Journal Avantscene*;[26] and two early examples appear in Motteroz's *Essai*, one made by Lefman, the other by Yves & Barret. The latter became one of the principal makers of line blocks in France.[27] The most celebrated book to use gillotage in France was Francesco de Quevedo's *Pablo de Segovia*, 1882, illustrated by Vierge,[28] but the process had previously been used in Doré's *Ariosto*, 1879[29] and A. Jacquemart's *Histoire du Mobilier*, Paris, 1876.[30] The latter was translated into English by Mrs B. Paliser as *A History of Furniture* and published by Chapman & Hall in 1878; it has line blocks in the text signed Gillot and must be one of the earliest English books to contain them.

Carl Hentschel (1869–1920), the original of 'Harris' in *Three Men in a Boat*, 1889, and a popular and respected figure in the printing trade, had been in business as a photo-engraver since 1887. In 1899 his firm took over Meisenbach and became the largest process firm in London. He said that his father had experimented for many years to make photomechanical line blocks and eventually succeeded by using carbon tissue;[31] but

that an artist who has once accustomed himself to use a brush never goes back to pens.

The foregoing materials and pens are for the production of simple black line drawings on a white ground, and it is in this direction that I should advise the student to persevere and

A FIELD PATH.
Bitumen process.   (*Original* 7½ × 6½.)   [*See p.* 86.

cultivate himself. All the beauty and expressiveness of lines is only realised after long practice ; and, of the many ways of illustrating by line process, it is the best means of self-education, compared with which all others are flippant and inconsequent.

Still, with some truth it has been said that it is only by

A HANDBOOK OF ILLUSTRATION. 83

experiment that we learn to achieve distinction, and so after a
while we may indulge in experiments in other directions, and

A FIELD PATH.
Swelled gelatine. (*Original* 7½ × 6½.) [*See p.* 86.

try our hand at the various tricks which the ingenious have
placed within our reach. These will be described in Chapter
XI.

Plate 34 Line blocks comparing bitumen process with swelled
gelatine. A. Horsley Hinton, *A Handbook of Illustration* (1894).
Each 10 × 9cm

this method was very difficult to carry out effectively and was eventually abandoned in favour of Gillot's method. The first etcher to practise gillotage is said to have come over to England in 1876, and was still working for Hentschel in 1900; the former date ties in fairly well with the suggested date of 1879 for the effective start of commercial photo-engraving in London.[32] It is possible that this French photo-engraver may have been Chefdeville.[33] Hentschel said that the Gillot method was still in use in 1900.

A certain number of process workers were in the field before 1879, and the first blockmaking firm in England is said to have been Alfred Dawson's, at work in 1871[34] though not included in Kelly's *Post Office Directory of . . . Printers* for 1872, which lists only D. C. Dallas under the heading of photographic engravers. In the 1876 edition the Typographic Etching Company is listed, with Alfred and William Dawson as managing partners. Hentschel thought that J. Leitch & Company were the first process engravers, and said that they were later taken over by John Swain. They were followed by Catell & Company, set up by some of Leitch's former employees, Leitch appearing in the 1876 directory as a litho-zincographer, together with Dellagana & Company. Catell & Company do not appear until 1880. At the Caxton Centenary Exhibition in 1877 the firms showing relief blocks made photomechanically were the Typographic Etching Co, L. Warnerke, and Manning & Son. These firms appear to have been the pioneers in methods of printing that by the end of the century were affording work to at least the thirty-six firms listed under 'Automatic and Photographic Engravers'.

By 1886 the first books in English principally concerned with the manufacture of photomechanical relief blocks were appearing: the earliest seem to have been Josef Böck's *Zincography*, first published in German in the previous year and translated by E. Menken, and W. T. Wilkinson's *Photo-engraving on Zinc and Copper*, 1886.

Böck's book recommends two methods of making blocks— using paper sensitised with bichromated gelatine or with albumenised bichromate of potash. In the latter case a rather crude background could be applied by putting a piece of crêpe or lace between the pictorial matter and the light, the image having been previously printed on to the sensitised paper. On exposure a dark background would appear on the transfer sheet. Böck described only transfer methods of making line blocks and did not appear to understand very clearly the swelled gelatine method. He has a short chapter on printing in colour from photomechanical blocks, recommending that drawings should be made on lithographic stone and subsequently transferred on to zinc, a rather roundabout method.

Wilkinson's book was a considerable improvement on Böck's. He describes coating the zinc plate by using a whirler made from a carpenter's brace, and states that the negative was printed down directly on to the zinc for etching. He also describes the use of bitumen as the light-sensitive material, which called for twice the exposure time of the other method, but was less liable to damage the image from over exposure. He does not mention swelled gelatine.

Swelled gelatine was one of the principal methods of making line blocks, having been used in England as early as the 1870s by D. C. Dallas[35] and others. Both Poitevin and Pretsch had used this method on the continent. Bolas said that Dallas was the first to introduce it to the English market and refers to the blocks as 'phototypic' blocks. It is difficult to assign the introduction of swelled gelatine to any one individual. Pretsch seems due for the credit, but he failed to make it work commercially and did not use it for relief printing. Dallas used it, apparently successfully, but kept his method secret. He appears to have sensitised a sheet of gelatine supported on a glass base, exposed it under a negative for 10–20 minutes in sunshine, then left it for several hours in water, which caused its unexposed portions to swell. A plaster of paris cast was then taken and used to prepare a stearine (or gutta percha) cast, and an electrotype was made from the latter. When it was backed up with type metal and mounted type high, the electrotype could be used with letterpress. Large areas of white had to be removed with a router at an earlier stage.

Duncan C. Dallas had been Pretsch's managing partner in London in the Patent Photo Galvanographic Company, but they eventually quarrelled, since Dallas worked an intaglio process that he claimed was different from Pretsch's, but Pretsch claimed it was the same. They pursued their quarrel in the German photographic press. In the event Dallas does not seem to have been very successful in this branch of the business, but he did produce illustrations of a different sort in various publications. In 1894 he advertised dallastype, dallastint and chromo-dallastint in W. T. Wilkinson's *Photo-engraving*, but the only one of these that seems to have been used in books to any extent was dallastype, which was evidently a relief process. Some of the illustrations in Robert Dickson's *Introduction of Printing into Scotland*, 1885, were dallastypes, and they were also used in Dickson & Edmond's *Annals of Scottish Printing*, published by Macmillan & Bowes in 1890. Pulls from some of the blocks in the latter book were given to William Blades by Dallas and are now in a scrapbook in St Bride's printing library, London.

Dallas exhibited his methods at the International Inventions Exhibition in 1885, where he was awarded a silver medal. One of his examples was an illustration by Walter Crane for the *Dallastype Shakespeare*, which came out in parts, starting with *The Tempest* in 1893. It has a number of plates by Crane on tissue paper stuck on to card mounts, boxed with a title page; 650 sets were printed and the plates destroyed. *Two Gentlemen of Verona* appeared in 1894. There is no imprint other than Dallas', though the spine of the box is blocked with Dent's name and the *English Catalogue* assigns the publication to Redway, who published the text of *The Tempest*. The *Merry Wives of Windsor* was announced but does not seem to have appeared. Dallas also made blocks for some work of Caldecott's (Plate 35).

An interesting indication of the state reached in line-block printing can be found in a lecture given to the Society of Arts by J. Comyns Carr in the summer of 1882. He said that relief blocks had been in use for some years and continued: 'Their great merit where they are successful, is that they give us the absolute auto-

"A Check."

Plate 35 Dallastype of Caldecott sketch. A. Brothers, *Photography* (1899). 8 × 11cm

graph of the artist. The photographer here takes the place of the wood engraver, and allows the original draughtsman to speak for himself.' His enthusiasm for line blocks was somewhat tempered by the drawbacks from which they were thought to suffer. Photography was said to coarsen and exaggerate the work of the artist; it is difficult to see why it should, but this may have been due to photographic enlargement or reduction to which artists were unaccustomed. Carr thought that French process workers produced better work than English, and mentioned Gillot and Yves & Barret. 'In London there are by comparison only a limited number of printing firms which devote special attention to this class of work, and although the results obtained in these isolated cases are highly satisfactory, the production is, as a general rule, far more costly.' He mentioned Dawson's typographic etching as an attempt to overcome some of the disadvantages of other process methods, and it was also mentioned by Sir H. T. Wood in *Modern Method of Illustrating Books*, 1887, who said that it had produced a great deal of excellent work. This process may have been used for what are described as 'Typo-etchings in the text' in a prospectus for C. E. Robinson's *A Royal Warren or Picturesque Rambles in the Isle of Purbeck*, published by the Typographic Etching Company in 1882, which has line blocks very pleasantly arranged in the text and etchings by Alfred Dawson. There are some other intaglio plates, made by a process described in the preface as 'photograving': 'An ordinary photographic negative is taken from the artist's drawing which is then impressed by the action of light on the gelatinous substance, portions of which being subsequently dissolved away.' A relief mould was made from the gelatine and an electrotype prepared. A plate of Rochester Castle in J. S. Hodson's *Guide to Art Illustration*, 1884, is captioned 'Typo-etching by Alfred Dawson'. The process was, in fact, misnamed, not being an etching process at all. The artist drew directly on to a plate of brass coated with a thin film of white wax, or, if he did not wish to use this surface, his design could be transferred on to the plate. The lines of the drawing were removed with an etching needle, and their depth then increased by running molten wax over the surface of the plate with a special tool. It was found that, since the wax would not cover up the lines where the brass showed through, sufficient depth was obtained to enable the plate to be electrotyped. Hubert Herkomer, Randolph Caldecott and Thomas Kent are all said to have tried out this process.[36]

HALFTONE BLOCKS

For all their advantages, line blocks still suffered from the same drawback as wood engraving, that they could not effectively portray tones. A practicable method of reproducing tones in relief printing, however, was eventually achieved by using dots small enough not to be readily detected by the human eye and infinitely variable in size. This method had been suggested by Fox Talbot as early as 1852, but it was to be another thirty years before it was available commercially. A number of inventors gave their minds to the problem and some fairly successful results were being produced by the 1870s.[37] Leggotype, used in America, employed a cross-line screen, but was applied to lithographic printing and does not seem to have been used in England. Frederick Ives invented a method of relief printing using dots that were obtained by pressing a woodburytype or swelled gelatine block against grained paper, thus making a pattern on its surface. The size of the dots would be proportional to the thickness of the woodburytype. This method was used in America in various forms, but, although described by both Böck and Wood, does not seem to have been employed in England.

The method finally employed to produce the dots was to place a cross-line screen between the original picture and the negative that was to be employed in making the printing plate. The plate would then print a picture wholly made up of dots whose size was directly proportional to the amount of light passing through the negative at any one point. This was first done commercially in England by George Meisenbach, whose method was patented in 1882.[38] He first used a single-line screen that was rotated to a second position during exposure, but this was soon replaced with a cross-line screen in which parallel lines were etched on two sheets of glass, blackened by the application of a colouring medium and cemented securely together at right-angles. Such screens were difficult to make, and for many decades the best came from Louis & Max Levy of Philadelphia. Meisenbach halftones started appearing in English books during the 1880s, and, since he had managed to avoid giving many details in his patent, he was able to work it as a secret method certainly as late as 1887.[39]

A different method had been patented in England in 1882[40] by a Liverpool firm named Brown, Barnes & Bell, and given the name of 'luxotype'. A wire mesh was pressed into the surface of a photograph and a negative made from it under a strong oblique light, a method that had the effect of breaking up the tones. Although luxotypes are said to have been used in a local newspaper, they were probably inadequate for bookwork and had been abandoned by 1899.[41]

Another type of screen, patented by James Wheeler in 1897, was called the mezzograph screen, and occasional examples of illustrations made with it can be found in books published in the late 1890s. It produced a noticeably irregular pattern in the print.

HYALOGRAPHY

One obvious way of making prints, after the invention of photography, was to manufacture a drawn negative instead of using a camera; but despite its obvious attractions, this was done surprisingly little. It was seen at its most successful, artistically, in the *cliché-verre* prints made by continental artists like Corot, Millet, and Rousseau. Two processes of this nature are mentioned in Stannard's *Art Exemplar*—one called elliotype after its inventor, who proposed it in 1858 for the reproduction of works of art; and an earlier method, which Stannard attributed to 'Mr Havell' and took from Fielding's *Art of Engraving*, 1841 (p 103), that was said to produce the effect of a mezzotint but does not appear to have been put to practical use. The ever enterprising Imperial Printing Office at Vienna printed an illustration in the latter process in Alois Auer's *Der polygraphische Apparat*, 1853, under the name of hyalography. This name stuck to the process and illustrations made by it can be found from time to time, often put forward as something entirely new. G. Hancock of Hither Green, London, a photo-engraver, used the process in the 1880s, producing the plate that demonstrated hyalography in Hodson's *Art Illustration*, from an original by W. S. Coleman. Coleman was also responsible for some of the illustrations in an edition of Samuel Rogers' *The Pleasures of Memory*, published by Sampson Low and printed by Edmund Evans, which has a number of plates executed by hyalography, one of them by Samuel Palmer (Plate 36). The book is undated but is probably c 1865–75. A note states how the plates were made: 'The large illustrations are produced by a new method without the aid of an engraver. . . . The drawing is made with an etching needle or any suitable

PLEASURES OF MEMORY.

Mark yon old Mansion, frowning thro' the trees,
Whose hollow turret woos the whistling breeze.
That casement, arch'd with ivy's brownest shade,
First to these eyes the light of heav'n convey'd.
The mouldering gateway strews the grass-grown court,
Once the calm scene of many a simple sport ;

When nature pleas'd, for life itself was new,
And the heart promised what the fancy drew.
    See thro' the fractur'd pediment reveal'd,
Where moss inlays the rudely sculptur'd shield,
The martin's old, hereditary nest.
Long may the ruin spare it's hallow'd guest !

10

Plate 36 Hyalograph by Samuel Palmer for S. Rogers, *The Pleasures
of Memory.* 6 × 10cm

point, upon a glass plate spread with collodion. It is then photographed upon a prepared surface of wax, and from this an electrotype is formed in relief which is printed with the type.'

Another book using hyalographs was P. G. Hamerton's *Man in Art*, published by Macmillan in 1892, in which they have a plate mark and a slight grain. The process used was invented by Dujardin, who is said by Hamerton to have used it for scientific illustration. The glass was given a fine and even grain, after which the artist drew on it with a lead pencil, stump, or brush with diluted Indian ink. The drawing was then printed down on to a metal plate covered with a sensitised etching ground, and the plate was washed and etched after exposure. The results are impressive, showing fine tones, and it is likely that the process never came into common use simply because more straightforward methods of photomechanical reproduction were becoming available by this time.

THE INK-PHOTO

One successful process used to quite an extent in bookwork was the ink-photo, the major users of which were Sprague & Company, a firm of lithographic printers of Fetter Lane, London, which had been founded in the early 1850s by Robert Winter Sprague. The firm introduced ink-photos as a secret process early in the 1880s, and an early example of its use is the frontispiece to H. K. F. Gatty's *Juliana Horatia Ewing and Her Books*, 1885—an odd choice as the original is entirely in line, and better adapted to the heliogravure process by which it is reproduced in some copies. Sprague's exhibited ink-photos at the International Inventors Exhibition in 1885, and they were used for some of the illustrations in John Charles Mackay's *Light Railways*, published by Crosby Lockwood in 1896, and to illustrate *The Builder* and *The Architect* for some years.

Ink-photos were basically collotypes,[42] made initially on a surface of reticulated gelatine on a glass base. The fineness of the grain could be determined by the thickness of the gelatine film— the thinner the film the finer the grain. A negative was exposed on to the gelatine in the usual way and a printing surface obtained. Instead of being printed, however, a transfer was made and used to make a lithographic printing surface from which the actual impressions were taken. Coloured ink-photos were also made, possibly by producing the actual colour stones direct and printing them on to a reticulated key. Other printers were using similar methods, though most of them date from the 1890s. Vincent Brooks, Day & Son were using screened keys, applying the colours from litho stones drawn by hand and achieving the tones by stippling. They made the plates for J. Inglis' *Tent Life in Tigerland*, 1892, in this way (Plate 37). A similar method, which lasted for a few years, was called 'wharf-litho'.[43]

PEN DRAWING

The end of this decade was marked by the publication in 1889 of *Pen Drawing and Pen Draughtsmen* by Joseph Pennell, an American book illustrator who spent much of his life in Europe, and is chiefly remembered for his *Lithography and Lithographers*, 1915. He spent his last years in America, not caring very much for what he found there after World War I, and embittered by failure to achieve recognition in the form of the medals and decorations which he hankered after. He was an enthusiast for photomechanical printing methods and wrote the introduction to the English edition of *Pablo de Segovia* in 1892. He had had some unfortunate experiences with wood engravers in his youth in America; on one occasion his drawing of a field of daisies had been turned into a river, the engraver excusing himself on the grounds that reproducing the daisies would ruin his eyesight![44] According to Pennell, pen drawing began to flourish about 1880, and its use in book illustration may well have been due to the successful development of techniques for transferring artists' drawings to wood photographically.

The illustrations in *Pen Drawing* were carried out by a wide variety of processes and firms, many of them not English. It had wood engravings and process blocks by J. Swain, and wood

Vincent Brooks, Day & Son Ltd

Plate 37 Chromolithograph with screened key and three tint stones by Vincent Brooks, Day & Son. J. Inglis, *Tent Life in Tigerland* (1892). 10·5 × 17cm

engravings by Edmund Evans and J. D. Cooper; process blocks were also provided by Walker & Boutall,[45] A. & C. Dawson, and Waterlow & Sons. Continental firms were represented by Gillot, Yves & Barret, Angerer & Göschl, and Meisenbach for relief work; Dujardin, Amand-Duran and the Berlin Photographic Company for intaglio; and others. It is appropriate that a book summing up, as it were, the state of reproductive book-illustration processes should have been published at the end of the decade in which photomechanical printing finally triumphed over hand methods.

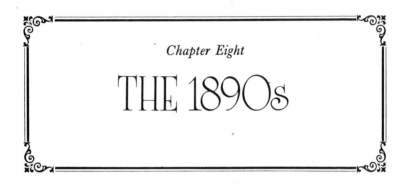

Chapter Eight

THE 1890s

ART NOUVEAU AND THE AESTHETIC MOVEMENT

BY THE 1890s all the technical innovations of lasting importance had been made in picture printing, with the exception of three-colour halftone. There was, doubtless, an increase in the number of photographic illustrations and a proportional decrease in original artists' work; one significant field in which artists' work was still of importance, however, was the movement known as Art Nouveau, though it is difficult to say how great its influence was on commercial book production. Art Nouveau was influenced by the Aesthetic Movement,[1] which started as far back as the 1860s with the work of a small number of architects and designers, and by the 1880s had come to influence book illustration. Amongst its characteristics were the use of certain colours, particularly greens and yellows, a noticeable style of dress and interior decoration, and Queen Anne architecture. The movement particularly influenced the children's picture books printed by

Edmund Evans. The first of the illustrators who drew for these books and were under the influence of the movement was Walter Crane (1845–1915), whose work was much influenced by Japanese colour prints, the style of which he used to a certain extent in his work for children. His work was published in 6d toy books in the 1860s and 1870s and larger 1s books after 1874. His most successful works were the *Baby's Opera*, 1877, the *Baby's Bouquet*, 1878, and the *Baby's Own Aesop*, 1887, but these were not published as toy books. In the *Aesop* the outlines were printed from photomechanical blocks and the colours from wood blocks. Crane said[2] that Kate Greenaway's *Under the Window* was published because he would not produce a repeat of the *Baby's Opera*, and this started her success from 1878. She was another representative of the Aesthetic Movement, and languid women in loose flowing draperies and sad children populate the pages of her books (Plate 38). Randolph Caldecott was the best artist of the three; his illustrations, starting with *The Three Jovial Huntsmen* in 1878, have been called 'in reality works of art imbued with subtle charm and rare originality'.[3] Both Caldecott and Crane did work for adult books as well as for picture books.

Children's books represented only part of Evans' colour output, for he also made colour prints for adult books and produced the coloured covers for yellow backs. In his *Reminiscences* he does not speak of electrotypes, and it seems possible that colour printers used the original wood blocks. Perhaps the standards of skill were higher among printers specialising in this kind of work.

The origins of Art Nouveau have been traced as far back as the work of Blake,[4] but it owed most to Japanese influences and the Aesthetic Movement. Some of the earliest Art Nouveau book illustration is associated with the work of A. H. Mackmurdo and the Century Guild *Hobby Horse*, founded in 1882;[5] but the most important book illustrator in the movement was Aubrey Beardsley. His first illustrations were for an edition of *Le Morte d'Arthur*, 1893, planned by J. M. Dent, who intended to produce a Kelmscott style book commercially. He was looking for illustrations in the style of Burne-Jones without having to pay that artist's high

Girls and boys come out to play,
The moon it shines as bright as day ;
Leave your supper, and leave your sleep,
And come to your playmates in the street ;
Come with a whoop, come with a call,
Come with a good will, or come not at all ;
Up the ladder and down the wall,
A halfpenny loaf will serve us all.

Plate 38   Relief colour print by Edmund Evans of a drawing by Kate
Greenaway. *Mother Goose* (1881)

fee, but got something rather different from, and in many ways superior to, the sort of medieval pastiche that was so attractive to Morris. The layout of the page of *Le Morte d'Arthur*, with floral borders round the pictures, is obvious imitation Kelmscott, but the pictures inside have more originality and a macabre spirit which is typical of Beardsley and far removed from the gentle romanticism of Kelmscott.

Beardsley went on to produce many other book illustrations, and their impact was very considerable, particularly in view of his short working life—he died in 1898. His work was significant in that it was intended to be reproduced photomechanically, and it is fortunate that it should have been artistically outstanding as well. It is evident from Beardsley's correspondence with his publishers, John Lane and Leonard Smithers,[6] that he fully appreciated the way in which his work was to be reproduced, for he often refers to the Swan Electric Engraving Company and Carl Hentschel, both of whom seem to have enjoyed his confidence. He recognised that different styles of drawing were needed for reproduction by halftone blocks and photogravure, and understood the relative expense of the different processes. His work was well suited to reproduction by line block, though Smithers was not a wealthy publisher, and most of his work may have been printed in this way because it was the cheapest.[7] Although wood engraving lingered on after Beardsley's time, it would hardly have been suited to his style, which obtained its tonal effects with intricate dotted patterns, and can be seen at its most elaborate in *The Rape of the Lock*, 1896. Beardsley thus represents the triumph of the new photomechanical methods over the old methods based on wood engraving.

Another significant figure in book production during the 1890s was William Morris, whose Kelmscott Press started work in 1891. He believed that good design could only be achieved by a return to the hand methods of the Middle Ages, and he produced hand-printed books (though not actually printed by himself) on hand-made paper—the result being expensive books. So far as illustration was concerned, Morris went back to the mid-nineteenth century rather than the Middle Ages since his illustrations were wood engravings produced in the classic nineteenth-century way. In the *Chaucer*, for example, published in 1896, Burne-Jones made drawings which were copied by Catterson Smith and cut by W. E. Hooper.[8] Morris influenced typography more than illustration, for, with the latter, he was fighting the inevitable trend towards photomechanical printing.

Apart from Beardsley, another pioneer in commercial line-block illustration was Hugh Thomson, whose work was reproduced first in this way in Macmillan's *English Illustrated Magazine* in April 1886. The illustrations were to *Days with Sir Roger de Coverley*, which appeared in book form in the same year.[9] Thomson went on to illustrate a number of other successful books, such as *The Vicar of Wakefield*, 1890, and *Cranford* in 1891, the latter giving its name to a series of illustrated books published by Macmillan that lasted until 1907. A number of other illustrators worked on this series, the most important of them being E. J. Sullivan. The success of the series led other publishers to copy it, making the illustrated series a distinctive, if minor, feature of the book world in the 1890s.[10]

SCRATCHBOARD

During the 1880s various attempts had been made to improve the tone values of relief blocks other than by the use of the cross-line screen, and these, though obsolescent, were used to some extent during the 1890s. One of the earliest was scratchboard, which was marketed in Britain by Maclure & Macdonald as early as 1870.[11] Scratchboard was card treated to produce an uneven surface—white board had impressed lines and black board had printed lines or patterns—and tone was achieved by scraping away the pattern with a special knife: by light scraping the lines could be converted into dots, and more vigorous scraping removed the dots to make areas of white. The drawing had, of course, to be made on the board before the tones were scraped in (Plate 39). The finished drawing was used to make a line block, or, before these were practicable, a lithographic transfer.

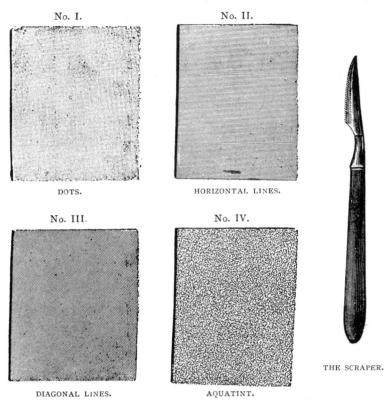

Plate 39 Scraperboard patterns in Horsley Hinton's *Handbook of
Illustration* (1894)

Similar effects could be obtained by using rough-surfaced paper
such as Conté, Allongé, Ingres, or Lalanne. Pyramid grained
paper had a granulated surface that formed dots whose size in
the finished drawing depended on the pressure used with a soft
pencil.[12] A reticulated pattern was also obtainable by splatter
work—dots of ink sprayed on to certain areas of the picture[13]
(Plate 40).

TRADE JOURNALS

The growth of photomechanical printing towards the end of the
century led to the foundation of periodicals dealing with its

NEAR BERRY HEAD.
Pen drawing—foreground dotted by " splatter" work. (*Original* 6½ × 5.)

Plate 40   Splatter work in Hinton's *Handbook* (1894)

processes and techniques. *The Process Photogram* was started in January 1895 as an offshoot of the photographic periodical *The Photogram*, which had been founded the previous year; *Penrose's Pictorial Annual* was also started in 1895, though that was not strictly speaking a periodical. Both these publications contained articles on the artistic and technical aspects of blockmaking by various processes and of printing the blocks. A more general periodical, dating from slightly earlier, was the *British Printer*, which had started in 1888. It was the journal of the 'British Typographia', an association of master printers and their employees that stemmed originally from the movements known as 'artistic printing' and 'antique printing', which had their origins in the 1870s and coalesced at the Caxton Exhibition in 1877. The chief exponent of 'antique' was Andrew Tuer, whose illustrative work is characterised by a conscious archaism such as the use of deliberately crude woodcuts. A good example of his style is *Old London Street Cries* . . . *with Heaps of Quaint Cuts*, 1885, published at the Leadenhall Press,[14] which combines reprints of early nineteenth-century and contemporary illustrations.

The *British Printer*, however, was firmly in the hands of the 'artistic' school, and among those concerned with the production of the first number was George W. Jones, a foreman at Raithby, Lawrence & Co, a Leicester printing firm. 'Artistic' printing and its development, the 'Leicester Free Style', were principally concerned with type and decoration in a conscious attempt to improve standards of printing by practising printers, but in the event this was only to be achieved when printing design was taken away from printers and given to designers. One significant but unappreciated fact about this movement was its enthusiasm for photomechanical illustration methods;[15] the *British Printer* used a good deal of process work for its illustrations. The movement was attempting to achieve the same ends as Morris, though looking forwards instead of backwards, and trying to raise the standards of the new processes and to integrate them into letterpress printing. By the end of the century they had not really succeeded, however, partly because very low standards of artistic work were commercially acceptable then; the 1890s, in fact, was the period in which the 'chocolate box' style of art reached its zenith. But if these periodicals failed in their artistic mission, they succeeded on the technical level in showing the genesis of relief printing in colour by halftone.

COLOUR HALFTONE

Colour printing from relief halftone blocks can hardly be considered to have been a commercially practicable printing method before the very end of the century. The theory of trichromatic printing, which was to be the eventual solution of the problem was known for a considerable time before it was physically possible to put it into practice. The first suggestion for printing in this way was made as early as 1861, but techniques were not far enough advanced for use to be made of it.[16] A number of workers advanced the theory, but the first person actually to make a trichromatic relief print seems to have been F. E. Ives in 1881.[17] One essential prerequisite was the invention of the cross-line screen and it was this which enabled a number of workers to produce effective results from the theories. It was a mistaken faith in the theory which led to one of the most important drawbacks in early attempts at this method of printing: if the three primary colours printed over one another theoretically produced black, the blockmakers could see no reason why it should not do so in practice. C. G. Zander, writing about Vogel's method of trichromatic printing, said: 'The system . . . necessitated the use of a grey tint, which is not necessary if the process is carried out on strictly scientific principles.' Unfortunately, whatever the principles may say, a colour halftone looks infinitely better with a fourth printing in black, and its absence accounts for the lack of definition in early colour work.

There were two methods of making screened colour plates in relief during the 1890s, but one of them, involving considerable handwork, gave way during the decade to a second, purely photographic, method. In the former system a key tracing was first made, followed by negatives for the tone block and the key block; and these were then exposed on metal for etching in the usual way. Set-offs were made for the colour blocks, the appropriate coloured areas being drawn in by hand on the separate blocks. Sometimes Day's shading mediums were used (they were patterns embossed on gelatine which could be transferred to the surface of the block). Thus, in this method a screened outline was obtained and one block for each colour, and often more than three were used.

In the photographic method three negatives were made by using filters to produce yellow, red and blue printings. From these a further set of negatives was made through the Levy screen, printed down on the metal and etched to make the blocks.[18] This method was technically more involved but was ultimately to prove the more effective of the two, and was greatly improved when it was realised that the screen could be inserted at the colour separation stage, though it is unlikely that this happened before the twentieth century.[19]

It was the tradition, as it still is, for coloured process prints not to be signed by the blockmaker, so it is difficult to follow the growth of this sort of illustration in commercially published books. Fortunately the trade periodicals published coloured prints, and, since they were primarily addressed to the trade, their plates were probably as up to date as their manufacturers could make them; they must also have been commercially available since they were virtually advertisements. The *British Printer* for 1891 has a number of plates made with the screened key and tint blocks by E. T. W. Dennis of Scarborough and Hare & Company, and one with a screened outline and flat colours by Meisenbach. Hare's were wood engravers who had turned over to process work in the mid 1880s; they called their colour work 'chromotypography'. Their prints appeared once again in the *British Printer* for 1892, which also contained some illustrations printed direct from relief blocks without a screen by Waterlow & Sons, who called them 'chromo-typographic' blocks. Other firms said to have been at work in this field by this year were the Photochromatic Printing Co of Belfast and Gilbert Whitehead & Co.[20] By 1893 a number of firms were represented in the *British Printer* by unscreened grained blocks, including Meisenbach and Hare & Co. Raithby, Lawrence, the printers of the periodical, advertised electros of grained blocks for colour printing. In this volume a genuine trichromatic print appeared, described as 'Photochromotypy in three workings', by Husnik & Häusler of Prague. They had an English agent in London through whom presumably they hoped to market these prints. An interesting but probably unusual example in this volume is a colour print in eight tints from Gilby & Herrmann's photo process boards, but elaborate colour work of this nature from scraperboard does not seem to have been particularly common.

Husnik & Häusler were again represented in the 1894 *British Printer* with trichromatic screened prints, one of which, accompanied by separate impressions of the three blocks, makes an interesting comparison with another print, by Angerer & Göschl of Vienna, made by the screen key and grain block method and also printed with separate impressions of the tone and grain blocks. Six blocks were used in this case and the results were considerably more attractive than Husnik & Häusler's. In an interesting article in this volume on the Meisenbach Company the managing director, W. P. Dilworth, said that three-colour process was 'scarcely in a commercial condition' and the evidence seems to bear him out; though it was to become commercially successful in the next two or three years. In the 1895 volume the Heliochrome Company and Hare both had trichromatic screened prints, though the majority of the coloured illustrations were of the screen and grain variety.

Hare & Co printed a supplement to the *Photogram* in 1895 in their 'photochromotypy', showing progressive printings of the screened key and three grained blocks. In 1896 a three-colour screened print was included, as was an example of 'synchromie', an invention of Count Turati. All the colours of the latter were printed at one impression, with a screened key printed in a separate impression, a system probably commercially impracticable. In 1898 one three-colour screened print by Carl Hentschel appeared, and in 1899 another, together with one by Thomas Huson. The latter is particularly interesting as separate progressive prints were also included.

By far the greatest number of colour prints appeared in *Penrose's Annual*, in which the triumph of the three screened blocks is well demonstrated. Among those whose productions appeared up to 1899 were the Heliochrome Company, Waterlow, Husnik & Häusler, Arthur Cox, John Swain and Bemrose. One surprise is Ernest Nister, whose best known work in the elaborate children's books of the 1890s is generally screened on the monochrome pages and grained on the colour prints.

It seems probable that the key and tint block method was commercially available from the start of the 1890s. Its popularity may have been due to blockmaking firms finding it easier to recruit printers experienced in making separations by hand than competent photographers. By about 1895 the three-colour process was commercially available from a number of blockmakers,[21] even if it was not used much for bookwork. It is perhaps significant that even books specifically about illustration, like H. Blackburn's *The Art of Illustration*, 1894, and J. Verfasser's *The Half-tone Process*, 1894 and 1896, had no colour plates until their post 1900 editions. The arrival of the colour halftone conveniently coincided with the work of Edmund Dulac and Arthur Rackham in the early twentieth century. Their significance lies in being the first books with coloured process illustrations which are collected for the plates. Martin Hardie wrote in *English Coloured Books*: 'It can be understood that a collector may treasure an aquatint, a chromolithograph, a coloured wood engraving, but a process plate never.' He wrote this in the year that Rackham's *Rip van Winkle* appeared, 1905, and this book was to be one of those that proved Hardie wrong, although he had logic on his side; the illustrations are quite ordinary three-colour plates by Carl Hentschel. The high prices commanded by Rackham's books must be partially due to careful marketing by his publishers, who manufactured rarity by issuing special limited editions.

C. T. Jacobi, writing in the early 1900s,[22] said: 'Within the last few years illustrated books have become more and more frequent, until at the present time very few books are published without some kind of illustration. . . . The facility with which illustrations can be produced is largely responsible for this tendency; the demand for "pictures" in a book has undoubtedly stimulated the development of modern methods of engraving.' Allowing for some exaggeration this sums up rather well the state of affairs at the end of the century. The search for tone had been brought to a successful conclusion and it could be produced in a number of ways. As might be expected, the more expensive ways were better than the cheaper; Jacobi listed them in ascending order of cost as line process, halftone, collotype, and photogravure.

Above all, the exactly repeatable image, accurately delineating any artifact, was available at a price within the means of a substantial proportion of the population. For the first time it was possible for the ordinary person to see different parts of the world as they were, and the first major step in the 'shrinking world', which was to be such a feature of twentieth-century civilisation, had been taken.

APPENDIX

*Frequency of Use of Different Illustration
Methods 1850–1900*

THIS SURVEY of the methods by which books were illustrated between 1850 and 1900 was based on those books in the Bodleian Library classified as 'art', since this group seemed the most likely to be well illustrated. There are about 1,200 of them. Books were broadly classified by subject for convenience in shelving in the library after 1850. They were also classified by size and arranged by shelfmark in the order in which they were acquired. A new series of shelfmarks was started in 1883, and the books are in fact kept in several different sequences on two floors in the stacks under the New Bodleian. The books counted were those in English published in England, and either dated in the imprint or by Bodley's date stamp, though the latter was not introduced until 1883. For the purposes of the survey the books were counted by decades and the results expressed as percentages of the total number of books in each decade. The figures can be seen on the diagram in which each decade is separated from the next by the scale on the left-hand side.

One feature that complicated the results was the use of two or more different illustration methods in one book, which varied from a low of 6·5 per cent of the sample in the 1860s to a high of 29·8 per cent in the 1890s. Since it was not practicable to count one book twice or more, the predominating illustrative method is considered to be the only one.

The diagrams are arranged with the relief processes on the left, followed by intaglio, then planographic and finally photographic methods on the right. In the last two decades photomechanical line blocks and wood engravings have been put together as 'line illustrations', since it is not possible to tell them apart with any certainty. Similarly photogravures and heliogravures have been counted together under the title 'photo intaglio'.

While this survey is only a sample, it is the first attempt to assess Victorian illustration methods quantitatively, and several interesting patterns emerge. Although wood engraving was the most popular method of illustration, it never exceeded 30 per cent of the total and was closely pursued by lithography. Chromolithography seems always to have been a minor form of reproduction, at its most popular in the 1850s and declining slowly through the rest of the century. One very significant figure is the 2 per cent of photographs in the 1850s, increasing to nearly 15 per cent in the 1860s. The revival of etching can be seen in the 1870s and 1880s. Screened halftones start to appear in the 1880s and rapidly became the most popular method in the 1890s.

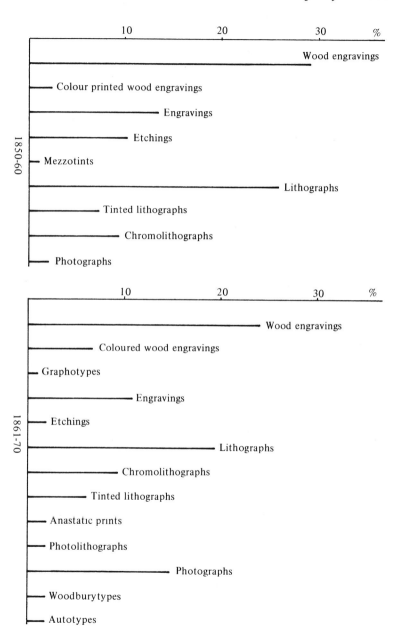

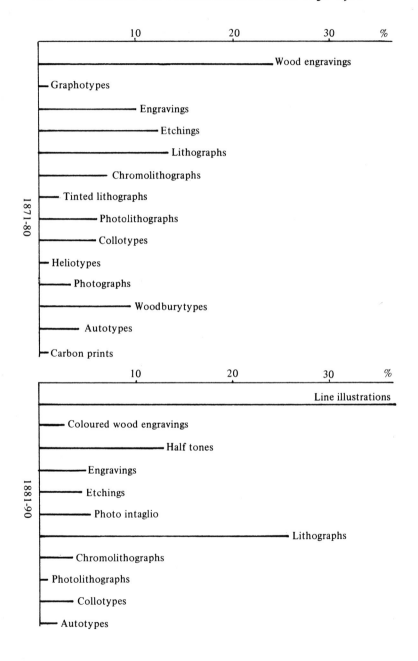

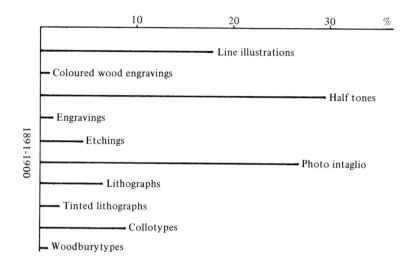

LIST OF WORKS CONSULTED

All published in London unless otherwise specified

CONTEMPORARY

Auer, A. *Der polygraphische Apparat* (Vienna, 1853)

Bigmore, E. C. & Wyman, C. W. *A Bibliography of Printing* (1880)

Blackburn, H. *The Art of Illustration* (1894)

Böck, J. *Zincography* [c 1886]

Bolas, T. 'The Application of Photography to the Production of Printing Surfaces and Pictures in Pigment', *JSA* (1878)

——. 'Recent Improvements in Photo-mechanical Printing Methods', *JSA* (1884)

——. 'Cylinder and Rotary Machine Printing for Photo-engraved . . . Plates', *Penrose Annual* (1897)

Brothers, A. *Photography: Its History, Processes, Apparatus, and Materials* (1899)

Burton, W. K. *Practical Guide to Photographic and Photo-mechanical Printing* (1892)

Carr, J. C. 'Book Illustration Old and New', *JSA* (1882)

Caxton Celebration, 1877. *Catalogue of the Loan Collection connected with the Art of Printing* (1877)

Dalziel, G. & E. *The Brothers Dalziel, 1840–90* (1901)

Denison, H. A. *A Treatise on Photogravure in Intaglio by the Talbot-Klič Process* [1895]

Fielding, T. H. *The Art of Engraving* (1844)

Gould, J. *The Letter-press Printer* (1893)

Great Exhibition. *Official Descriptive and Illustrative Catalogue* (1851)

——. *Reports by the Juries* (1852)

Grupe, E. Y. *Instructions in the Art of Photographing on Wood* (Leominster, Mass, 1882)

Hamerton, P. G. *The Graphic Arts* (1882)

Head, Sir F. B. 'The Printer's Devil', *Quarterly Review*, vol 65 (1839–40)

Hentschel, C. 'Process Engraving', *JSA* (1900)

Hinton, A. H. *A Handbook of Illustration* (1894)

Hodson, J. S. *An Historical and Practical Guide to Art Illustration* (1884)

Hunt, R. 'On the Application of Science to the Fine and Useful Arts . . . Steel Plates for Engraving', *Art Journal* (1850)

Jackson, J. & Chatto, W. A. *A Treatise on Wood Engraving* (1839)

Jacobi, C. T. *Some Notes on Books and Printing* (1902)

——. *The Printers' Handbook* (1905)

Joyner, G. *Fine Printing, Its Inception, Development and Practice* (1895)

Linton, W. J. *Wood Engraving* (1884)

Motteroz, C. *Essai sur les Gravures Chimique en Relief* (Paris, 1871)

Nolte, V. *Memorial of Facts connected with the History of Medallic Engraving and the Process of M. Collas* (1838)

Ordnance Survey. *Account of the Methods and Processes adopted for the Production of the Maps of the Ordnance Survey of the U.K.* (1875 and 1902)

Pennell, J. *The Illustration of Books* (1889)

Poole, W. *Life of Sir William Siemens* (1888)

Sawyer, J. R. *The Autotype Process* (1873)

Scott, A. de C. *On Photo-zincography* (1863)

Singer, H. W. & Strang, W. *Etching, Engraving, and Other Methods of Printing Pictures* (1897)

Sketchley, R. E. D. *English Book Illustration of Today* (1903)

Smee, A. *Elements of Electrometallurgy* (1843)

Smillie, T. W. 'Photographing on Wood for Engraving', *Smithsonian Miscellaneous Collections*, Washington, DC, vol XLVII (1905)

Southward, J. *Practical Printing* (1882)

———. *Principles and Progress of Printing Machinery* [c 1890]

Spencer, A. 'Vindication of Claims to Certain Inventions and Improvements in the Graphic Art', *American Journal of Science and Arts*, vol XLIV (1843)

Spencer, T. *Instructions for Multiplication of Works of Art . . .* (Glasgow, 1840)

Stannard, W. J. *The Art Exemplar* [c 1860]

Tomlinson, C. *Cyclopedia of Useful Arts and Manufactures* (1852)

Verfasser, J. *The Half-tone Process* (1896 and 1904)

Vogel, H. *The Chemistry of Light and Photography in Their Application to Art, Science and Industry* (1876)

Warren, C. 'Engraving on Steel Plate', *JSA* (1823)

West, W. *Fifty Years Recollections of an Old Bookseller* (1837)

White, G. *English Illustration. The Sixties, 1855–70* (1897)

Wilkinson, W. T. *Photo-engraving . . . and Photogravure* (1890)

———. *Photo-engraving and Photo-lithography in Line and Half-tone also Collotype and Heliotype* (1888)

———. *Photo-engraving, Photolithography and Collotype* (1890)

Wilson, F. J. F. *Stereotyping and Electrotyping* (1880)

———. *Typographic Printing Machines and Machine Printing* (1879)

Wood, Sir H. T. *Modern Methods of Illustrating Books* (1887)

Zander, C. G. *Photo-trichromatic Printing* (1896)

MODERN

Abbey, J. R. *Scenery of Great Britain and Ireland in Aquatint and Lithography, 1770–1860* (1952)

Bain, I. 'Thomas Ross & Son', *JPHS* (1966)

Balston, T. 'English Book Illustration, 1880–1900', in J. Carter's *New Paths in Book Collecting* (1934)

——. 'Illustrated Series of the Nineties: the Cranford Series', *Book Collectors Quarterly*, vol XI (1933)

Beardsley, A. *Letters*, ed H. Maas and others (1970)

Beckett, R. B. 'Constable as an Illustrator', *The Connoisseur*, vol CXXIV (1955)

Berry, W. T. & Poole, H. E. *Annals of Printing* (1966)

Bland, D. *A History of Book Illustration* (1958)

Burch, R. M. *Colour Printing and Colour Printers* (1910)

Carter, H. *Orlando Jewitt* (1962)

Carter, J. *Binding Variants, 1820–1900* (1932)

Dreyfus, J. & Strouse, N. H. *C-S the Master Craftsman* (Michigan, 1969)

Eder, J. M. *History of Photography* (New York, 1945)

Evans, E. *The Reminiscences of Edmund Evans*, ed R. McLean (1967)

Fildes, P. 'Photo-transfer of Drawings in Woodblock Engraving', *JPHS* (1969)

Gernsheim, H. & A. *The History of Photography* (1969)

Gray, B. *The English Print* (1937)

Hardie, M. *English Coloured Books* (1906)

——. *Water-colour Painting in Britain* (1968)

Harris, E. 'Experimental Graphic processes in England, 1800–1859', *JPHS* (1968–9)

Ivins, W. M. *Prints and Visual Communication* (Cambridge, Mass, 1953)

James, P. *English Book Illustration 1800–1900* (1947)

Kainen, J. 'The Development of the Half-tone Screen', *Smithsonian Report for 1951* (Washington, DC, 1952)

Lewis, C. T. C. *The Story of Picture Printing in England during the Nineteenth Century* (1928)

Lindley, K. *The Woodblock Engravers* (Newton Abbot, 1970)

McLean, R. *Victorian Book Design and Colour Printing* (1963)

Mertle, J. S. 'The Evolution of Rotogravure', *Gravure* (1956–7)

Muir, P. H. *Victorian Illustrated Books* (1971)

Oxford Almanack, 1674–1946, The (New York, 1946)

Pennell, J. *The Adventures of an Illustrator* (1925)

Reid, F. *Illustrators of the Sixties* (1928)

Ridler, V. 'Artistic Printing, a Search for Principles', *Alphabet & Image* (1948)

Schultze, R. S. 'Books Illustrated with Original Photographs', *Jubiläums Festschrift Hundert Jahre Photographische Gesellschaft in Wien* (Vienna, 1961)

——. *Victorian Book Illustration with Original Photographs* (1962)

Stevens, J. 'Woodcuts dropped into the Text', *Studies in Bibliography*, vol XX (1967)

Stoyle, F. W. 'Michael Faraday and Anastatic Printing', *British Ink Manufacturer*, vol VIII (1965)

S[wan], M. E. & K. R. *Sir Joseph Wilson Swan* (1929)

Taylor, J. R. *The Art Nouveau Book in Britain* (1966)

Thomas, D. B. *The Science Museum Photography Collection* (1969)

Thorpe J. *English Illustration: the Nineties* (1934)

Threlfall, J. 'Fifty Years of Photogravure', *British Printer* (1945)

Twyman, M. *Lithography 1800–1850* (1970)

Victoria & Albert Museum. *The Great Exhibition of 1851* (1950)

Wakeman, G. *Aspects of Victorian Lithography* (Wymondham, 1970)

——. 'Henry Bradbury's Nature-printed Books', *The Library* (1966)

——. *XIX Century Illustration, Some Methods used in English Books, Illustrated with Original Examples of the Processes* (Loughborough, 1970)

Wakeman, G. & Cave, R. *Typographia Naturalis* (Wymondham, 1967)

Abbreviations

JSA   *Journal of the Society of Arts*

JPHS   *Journal of the Printing Historical Society*

NOTES

Chapter One

1. Berry, W. T. & Poole, H. E. *Annals of Printing* (1966), 258
2. Wilson, F. J. F. *Typographic Printing Machines* (1879), 45
3. *British Printer*, vol 7 (1894), 84. Wilson, C. H. & Reader, J. 'Men and Machines' (1958), 43-4
4. He was possibly connected with S. B. Bolas and Co, 11 Ludgate Hill, London
5. 'Cylinder and Rotary Machine Printing for Photo-engraved . . . Plates', *Penrose Annual* (1897), 51
6. Derry, T. K. & Williams, T. L. *A Short History of Technology* (Oxford, 1960), 513

Chapter Two

1. Beckett, R. B. 'Constable as an Illustrator', *The Connoisseur*, CXXIV (1955)
2. Stevens, Joan, 'Woodcuts dropped into the Text', *Studies in Bibliography*, XX (1968), 113. Harvey, J. R. *Victorian Novelists and their Illustrators* (1970); Chapters 5 and 6 consider the relationship between Dickens and his illustrators in detail
3. Jackson J. & Chatto, W. A. *A Treatise on Wood Engraving* (1839), 721
4. Bolas, T. 'Stereotyping', *JSA*, XXXVIII (1890)

5. Fielding, T. H. *The Art of Engraving* (1841), 8
6. Bathe, G. & D. *Jacob Perkins* (Philadelphia, 1943), 88
7. The best account of his work as an illustrator is in P. H. Muir, *Victorian Illustrated Books* (1970)
8. Gray. B. *The English Print* (1937), 166
9. Ibid, 167–8
10. Stannard, W. J. *Art Exemplar*, 45–6. Stannard knew Lowry (p 84), who did not himself publish his inventions and is a very elusive figure
11. Patent No 12248 (1848)
12. Harris, E. 'Experimental Graphic Processes in England 1800–1859', *Journal of Printing Historical Society*, 4 (1968), 74
13. Raimbach, A. *Memoirs and Recollections* (1843), 8
14. Hunt, R. 'On the Application of Science to the Fine and Useful Arts . . . Steel Plates for Engraving', *Art-Journal* (1850), 230–2
15. Dr C. F. Waagen, Director of the National Gallery at Berlin, visited England in 1835 and referred to 'The landscapes of . . . Turner, who is known throughout Europe by his numerous, often very clever, compositions for annuals and other works, where they appear in beautiful steel engravings.' Hardie, M. *Water Colour Painting in Britain*, vol 2, ed D. Snelgrove and others (1967), 33
16. Fielding, T. H. *Art of Engraving*
17. Davenport,C. *Mezzotints* (1904), 185–6
18. Carter, J. *Binding Variants 1820–1900* (1932), 83
19. Twyman, M. *Lithography 1800–1850* (Oxford, 1970), 159–60
20. Burch, R. M. *Colour Printing and Colour Printers* (1910)
21. Twyman, M. *Lithography*, 145
22. West, W. *Fifty Years Recollections of an Old Bookseller* (1837), 200, states that Chapman & Co had a mill at Dartford for the preparation of zinc plates. Burch, R. M. *Colour Printing*, 188
23. 'The Printer's Devil', *Quarterly Review*, LXV (1840), 28–9
24. McLean, R. *Victorian Book Design* (1963), 139–40
25. Harris, E. *JPHS*, vol 5 (1969), 53

Chapter Three

1. Twyman, M. *Lithography 1800–1850* (1970), 209, 219
2. Jackson, P. J. *Tallis's Street Views* (1969), 21
3. Abbey, J. R. *Scenery of Great Britain and Ireland in Aquatint & Lithography* (1952), No 245
4. Poole, W. *Life of Sir William Siemens* (1888)
5. Ibid, 57–8
6. Wakeman, G. 'Anastatic Printing for Sir Thomas Phillipps', *Journal of the Printing Historical Society* (1969)
7. The book must be dated between 1862 and 1866, as the firm only worked under that name during those years
8. Wakeman, G. *Aspects of Victorian Lithography* (1970)

9. McLean, R. *Victorian Book Design* (1963), 79
10. They have been fully described in McLean's *Victorian Book Design*; C. T. C. Lewis's *The Story of Picture Printing in the XIX Century* (1928); and R. M. Burch's *Colour Printing & Colour Printers* (1910)
11. Wakeman, G. & Cave, R. *Typographia Naturalis* (1967), ch 2
12. Wakeman, G. 'Henry Bradbury's Nature Printed Books', *The Library* (1966)
13. Harris, E. 'Experimental Graphic Processes in England, 1800–1859', *JPHS* (1969)

Chapter Four

1. Gray, B. *The English Print* (1937), 127
2. James, P. *English Book Illustration 1800–1900* (1947), 7
3. Reitlinger, G. *The Economics of Taste*, vol 2 (1961), 143–74
4. Quoted in Forrest Reid, 41
5. Muir, P. H. *Victorian Illustrated Books* (1971), 130
6. Balston, T. 'English Book Illustration, 1880–1900', in Carter. J. *New Paths in Book Collecting* (1934)
7. When the bolts are left unopened, the presence of pinholes may denote a book printed on a power platen after the mid-1860s
8. Martin Hardie in *DNB*; Evans, E. *Reminiscences* (1967), xvi
9. *Practical Printing*, 569
10. *An Historical and Practical Guide to Art Illustration*, 209
11. The use of wax was first adopted at the foundry of Cassell, Petter & Galpin, 'now universally used in this country, although . . . gutta percha is almost exclusively used on the continent'. Wilson, F. J. F. *Stereotyping and Electrotyping* [1880]. The wax was coated with powdered black lead, an improvement made by Robert Murray, in use as early as 1841
12. Hodson, J. S. *Guide to Art Illustration* (1884): 'The original wood-cut should never be used at machine, but an electrotype should be obtained . . .'. Southward, J. *Practical Printing*, 4th ed (1892): 'Electrotypes are now so cheap, and so quickly obtained, that printing is seldom done from the wood engraving itself. The use of the original engraving in the forme has several disadvantages. . . . if any accident happens to it, the engraver must have it to repair . . . and this is very costly, while a new electro can be obtained for a few pence . . . wood is very apt to warp . . . and even to crack . . .'
13. 'Photographing on Wood for Engraving', *Smithsonian Miscellaneous Collections*, vol XLVII (1905), 497
14. Fildes, P. 'Phototransfer of Drawings in Wood-block Engraving', *JPHS*, 5 (1969), 93, for Luke Fildes selling his drawings after engraving. Hamerton, P. G. *Drawing and Engraving* (1892), 103, comments that engravers did not like the arrangement and it was the publishers and artists who encouraged it.

Chapter Five

1. Snow, Vernon F. 'The First Photographically Illustrated Book', *The Times Literary Supplement* (23 December 1965), 1204
2. Gernsheim, H. & A. *A History of Photography* (1969), 171–3
3. Ibid, 204
4. Ibid, 286
5. Schultze, R. S. 'Books Illustrated with Original Photographs', *Jubiläums Festschrift Hundert Jahre Photographische Gesellschaft in Wien* (1961), 144
6. Ibid, 139
7. Gernsheim. *History*, 546
8. Scott, A. de C. *Photozincography* (1862)
9. Vol 7, 163, 213
10. An account was published in the *Transactions of the Philosophical Institute* (Melbourne, 1859), 172–83
11. Gernsheim. *History*, 547
12. Wilkinson, W. T. *Photo-engraving and Photolithography*, 2nd ed [1888], 85: '. . . but although the patentees issued some fine specimens of their work and advertised the sale of prepared paper nothing came of it'.
13. Brothers, A. *A Manual of Photography* (1899), 156

Chapter Six

1. Gernsheim, H. & A. *A History of Photography* (1969), 337
2. Ibid, 338
3. Poitevin is said by Simpson to have used these prints in a book, *Premières Epreuves du Photographie au Charbon* in 1855, but I have been unable to trace a copy
4. W. Portbury, in *Photographic News* (23 November 1860) claimed he had made the invention while apprenticed to Pouncy
5. M.E. & K.R. S.[wan]. *Sir Joseph Wilson Swan* (1929), 37
6. Gernsheim. *History*, 339. Other inventors with the same idea were equally unsuccessful
7. Ibid, 339
8. Ibid, 340; Eder, J. M. *History of Photography* (New York), 558
9. *The Autotype Process*, 3rd ed (1873), 190
10. There is an undated example in the John Johnson Collection
11. *Bibliography of Printing*, vol 1, 190
12. Schultze, R. S. *Victorian Book Illustration with Original Photographs, Catalogue of an Exhibition at the National Book League* (1962)
13. Eder. *History*, 587
14. *Abridgement of Specifications* (1864), class 101, No 2338
15. Tangye Brothers of Queen Victoria Street, London, made presses suitable for this work for about £50
16. Gernsheim. *History*, 341

17. Burton, W. K. *Practical Guide to Photographic & Photo-mechanical Printing* (1887), 254–72
18. About 10,000 a week according to Tissandier's *History of Photography* (1878), 219, from one turntable
19. Gernsheim. *History*, 341
20. In Wilkinson's *Photo-engraving*, 5th ed
21. Eder. *History*, 588–9
22. By Eder and Gernsheim
23. Gernsheim. *History*, 547–8
24. According to Gernsheim
25. In *Photo-engraving* . . . *Collotype and Heliotype*
26. Schnauss, J. *Collotype and Photo-lithography* (1889)
27. Ibid, 163–5
28. Gernsheim. *History*, 549. Two letters from Edwards & Kidd to George Cruikshank are preserved in the John Johnson Collection. The first is dated 9 May 1870, and on it the firm are described as 'Licencees of the Autotype Co.'. On the heading of the second letter, dated 25 January 1871, this phrase is crossed out, so that it reads 'Edwards and Kidd, 22, Henrietta St., Covent Gdns. Printers of permanent photographs called heliotypes.' The last two words are written in ink
29. Gernsheim. *History*, 549, says this was the first book illustrated with them
30. *Colour Printing and Colour Printers* (1910), 226

Chapter Seven

1. Gernsheim, H. & A. *History of Photography* (1969), 57–8
2. Ibid, 543
3. *Journal of the Photographic Society* (May 1853), 64
4. Mertle, J. S. 'Evolution of Rotogravure', *Gravure* (April 1956), 21, prints reproductions of Talbot's etchings and his screen
5. Waterhouse, J. 'Paul Pretsch and Photo-galvanography', *Penrose Annual*, vol 16 (1910–11), 137–42; Gernsheim. *History*, 541–3; Mertle. *Gravure* (May 1956), 23
6. This was a swelled gelatine method. Eder. *History*, 586
7. Catalogue, 327
8. Hamerton, P. G. *Drawing and Engraving* (1892), 151–3. Dujardin also operated a complicated tone process invented by H. Garnier (see Eder. *History*, 595), but I have not seen any in English books. Mertle. *Gravure* (June 1956), 25–6
9. Mertle. *Gravure* (June 1956), 26
10. Ibid, 28
11. Wood. *Modern Methods of Illustrating Books* (1887), 204. Bolas, T. 'Recent improvements in Photo-mechanical Printing Methods', *JSA*, vol XXXII (October 1884), 1099
12. *Catalogue*, 329–30

13. Jacobi, C. T. *The Printers' Handbook*, 3rd ed (1905). Earlier editions do not include this process
14. Bolas. *JSA*, vol XXXII, 1101
15. Mertle. *Gravure* (July 1956)
16. Threlfall, John. 'Fifty years in Photogravure', *British Printer* (1945), 58
17. Christie, G. *Storeys of Lancaster 1848–1964* (1964), 100
18. Wilkinson, W. T. *Photo-engraving . . . and Photogravure*, 5th ed (1894), 141, recommends powdered resin and asphaltum in equal parts
19. Threlfall. *BP* (1945)
20. Hardie. *English Coloured Books*, 298
21. Carr, J. Comyns. 'Book Illustration Old and New', *JSA* (October 1882), 1056–7
22. *Penrose Annual* (1894), 90
23. Gernsheim. *History*, 543
24. *Annals of Printing*, 249
25. P 64
26. Eder, *History*, 622; Motteroz. *Essai . . .*, 71
27. Carr, J. Comyns. *JSA* (1882), 1060
28. A Spaniard whose real name was Daniel Urrabieta, 1851–1904. Malcolm Bell in Bryan's *Dictionary of Artists and Engravers* (1903–4), calls him 'the father of modern illustration'
29. Bland, D. *History of Book Illustration* (1958), 279
30. Howe, E. 'Bewick to the Half-tone', *Typography*, vol 3 (1937)
31. Carr, J. Comyns. *JSA* (1882), 1061–2
32. *Process Photogram* (1899), 95
33. Hentschel, C. 'Process Engraving', *JSA*, vol 48 (April 1900), 464; Pennell, J. *Pen Drawing and Pen Draughtsmen* (1889), 137
34. *Annals of Printing*, 249
35. Bolas, T. *JSA* (1878), 804
36. Pennell, J. *Pen Drawing* (1889), 292
37. Kainen, J. 'The Development of the Halftone Screen', *Smithsonian Report* (1951)
38. No 2156
39. Wood, Sir H. T. *Modern Methods*, 157
40. Nos 1380 and 4705
41. Wood, Sir H. T. *Modern Methods*, 162; Kainen, J. *Smithsonian Report*, 419; Brothers, A. *Photography* (1899), 122, says it had been abandoned
42. According to Wilkinson, W. T. *Photo-engraving and Photolithography* [1888], 86–94
43. Burch, R. M. *Colour Printing*, 218–19; *Process Photogram* (1899), 117
44. Pennell, J. *The Adventures of an Illustrator* (1925), 85
45. Emery Walker's firm. See Dreyfus, J. 'Cobden-Sanderson's Partnership with Emery Walker', in *C.S. the Master Craftsman* (Adagio Press, Michigan, 1969)

Chapter Eight
1. Aslin, E. *The Aesthetic Movement* (1969)
2. *Imprint* (February 1913), 84
3. Hardie, M. *Water-colour Painting in Britain*, III, *The Victorian Period* (1968), 109
4. Taylor, J. R. *The Art Nouveau Book in Britain* (1967), 9
5. Ibid, 34–7
6. *The Letters of Aubrey Beardsley*, ed Haas and others (1970)
7. Ibid, 404
8. James, P. *English Book Illustration* (1947), 56
9. Balston, T. 'English Book Illustration, 1880–1900', *New Paths in Book Collecting* (1934)
10. Ibid; Sketchley, R. E. D. *English Book Illustration of Today* (1905); and Thorpe, J. *English Illustration: the Nineties* (1935)
11. Eder. *History*, 625
12. Hinton, A. Horsley. *A Handbook of Illustration* [1894], 102–8
13. Ibid, 94–5
14. Ridler, Vivian. 'Artistic Printing: a Search for Principles', *Alphabet and Image*, 6 (1948), 9
15. Joyner, G. *Fine Printing* (1895), 19
16. Burch, R. M. *Colour Printing* (1910), 237
17. Zander, C. G. *Photo-trichromatic Printing* [1896], 35
18. Richmond, W. D. 'The Limitation of Three-colour Printing', *Penrose Annual* (1899), 25
19. Verfasser, J. *The Half-tone Process* (1904), 282
20. Burch, R. M. *Colour Printing*, 238
21. Hardie, M. *English Coloured Books* (1906), 296, says 1897
22. Jacobi, C. T. *Some Notes on Books and Printing* (1902), 33

INDEX

177